COHABITING MOTHERS

The Policy Studies Institute (PSI) is Britain's leading independent research organisation undertaking studies of economic, industrial and social policy, and the workings of political institutions.

PSI is a registered charity, run on a non-profit basis, and is not associated with any political party, pressure group or commercial interest.

PSI attaches great importance to covering a wide range of subject areas with its multi-disciplinary approach. The Institute's 50+ researchers are organised in teams which currently cover the following programmes:

Family Finances – Employment – Information Policy – Social Justice and Social Order – Health Studies and Social Care – Education – Industrial Policy and Futures – Arts and the Cultural Industries – Environment and Quality of Life

This publication arises from the Employment Studies programme and is one of over 30 publications made available by the Institute each year.

Information about the work of PSI, and a catalogue of available books can be obtained from:

Marketing Department, PSI
100 Park Village East, London NW1 3SR

The Joseph Rowntree Foundation has supported this project as part of its programme of research and innovative development projects, which it hopes will be of value to policy makers and practitioners. The facts presented and views expressed in this report, however, are those of the authors and not necessarily those of the Foundation.

Cohabiting Mothers

Changing marriage and motherhood?

Susan McRae

Policy Studies Institute
London

The publishing imprint of the independent
POLICY STUDIES INSTITUTE
100 Park Village East, London NW1 3SR
Telephone: 071-387 2171 Fax: 071-388 0914

© **Policy Studies Institute 1993**

ISBN 0 85374 571 4

A CIP catalogue record of this book is available from the British Library.

1 2 3 4 5 6 7 8 9

PSI publications are available from
BEBC Distribution Ltd
P O Box 1496, Poole, Dorset, BH12 3YD

Books will normally be despatched within 24 hours. Cheques should be made
payable to BEBC Distribution Ltd.

Credit card and telephone/fax orders may be placed on the following freephone
numbers:

FREEPHONE   0800 262260
FREEFAX   0800 262266

PSI subscriptions are available from PSI's subscription agent
Carfax Publishing Company Ltd
P O Box 25, Abingdon, Oxford OX14 3UE

Laserset by Policy Studies Institute
Printed in Great Britain by BPCC Wheatons Ltd, Exeter

Acknowledgements

I wish to thank both the Joseph Rowntree Foundation and the Department of Social Security for making this study possible. The Joseph Rowntree Foundation generously funded the project, and the DSS kindly enabled further access to respondents to the 1988 Maternity Rights Survey.

Interviews for the study were carried out by PAS Limited, under the direction of Ruth Lennox and Stuart Robinson. I am grateful to them both and to their teams of conscientious and skilled interviewers.

The bulk of the computer analyses were carried out at PSI by my colleague Chris Dawson; I am very grateful for her help and patience. I am indebted also to Lydia Maher who painstakingly compiled the quotations from respondents used in the text.

Members of the Joseph Rowntree Foundation project advisory group, chaired by Barbara Ballard, provided many valuable comments and I wish to thank all of them: Ceridwen Roberts, Mavis McLean, Kathleen Kiernan, Sharon Jones and Erica De'Ath.

Finally, of course, a debt of gratitude is owed to the 328 women who participated in the research. Without them, there would have been no study.

Susan McRae

Contents

Tables

1 Introduction

Not much more than a generation ago, onlookers at a wedding celebration might reasonably have assumed that the bride in white – if *not* her newly-acquired husband – was a virgin. An unmarried pregnancy was a source of great personal and family shame. Although pre-marital sex most certainly occurred, cohabitation outside of marriage and pre-marital births were rare. Love and marriage 'went together like a horse and carriage'; marriage and family were synonymous. Moreover, song lyrics expressed more than ideology: illegitimacy and cohabitation rates in the late 1950s were at their lowest points in more than a hundred years.[1]

Yet today, almost half of all conceptions occur outside marriage and 1 in 3 women give birth while unmarried, many choosing instead to live in consensual unions with the child's father. Indeed, since the 1960s, when love and marriage seemed suddenly to fly apart, the demographics of childbirth have changed rapidly. Women now have fewer children, later: mothers' average age at first birth has risen steadily, reaching 27.5 years in 1990, its highest point since 1961.[2] Since 1973 the birth rate has been below replacement level, at about 1.8 children per woman.[3] The rate of births outside marriage, which remained below 5 per cent until the 1950s, has leaped upwards, to 13 per cent in 1981 and to 30 per cent in 1991.[4] The births of children born outside marriage increasingly have been registered by both parents. Just under half of all births outside marriage in 1975 were jointly registered, rising to over two-thirds in 1987; 70 per cent of joint registrations in 1987 were made by parents who lived at the same address.[5]

Rates of marriage, divorce and of remarriage after divorce have also changed markedly. The marriage patterns of women born in 1946 were typical of those found among women born throughout the 1940s: 60 per cent married between the ages of 19 and 23 years, the median age at marriage was 21.5 years and 92 per cent married by age 30.[6] First marriages, moreover, accounted for 86 per cent of all marriages in 1961.[7]

Women born in 1958 and 1964 exemplify the changing patterns of marriage. The median age at marriage of women born in 1958 was 22.5 years, a gain of one year, while the proportion married by age 30 fell to 81 per cent. One in five marriages in 1971 included at least one partner

1

marrying for the second time. The median age at marriage among women born in 1964 rose yet again, to 25.5 years, and estimates suggest that only about 70 per cent are likely to marry by age 30 (in 1994).[8] Fewer marriages still in 1989 were first marriages for both participants, with over one-third (36 per cent) of all marriages including at least one previously-married partner.[9]

The decline in marriage rates came with a sharp increase in rates of cohabitation. It has been estimated that there were 1.2 million cohabiting couples in Britain in 1989, representing 1 in 12 of all couples.[10] From the mid-1960s when only a handful of couples lived together before marriage, until the late 1980s when over 50 per cent did so, cohabitation has grown to become common practice before marriage and virtually the norm before re-marriage.[11]

Generally, however, cohabitation in Britain *precedes* rather than *replaces* marriage, and seldom lasts beyond two or three years. Nonetheless, a growing number of couples are choosing not to marry before becoming parents. Estimates made in 1989 suggested that about 4 per cent of all dependent children lived in cohabiting families; that is, in families with both natural parents who were not married to each other.[12]

Cohabitation, and in particular, motherhood within cohabitation, challenges the long-standing ideal, common to Britain and many other industrialised societies, that has depicted marriage (and the traditional family unit) as the best – or only – place to have and rear children. We cannot predict the pace at which cohabiting relationships will increase, nor whether the length of time cohabiting couples remain together and unmarried will lengthen. From the foregoing discussion, however, it seems likely that the number of British couples living together in consensual unions will continue to increase steadily, and that many more cohabiting couples will have children. While only 1 in 10 18-24 year olds surveyed for the 1989 British Social Attitudes study would recommend *permanent* cohabitation, fewer than half thought that people should marry before having children.

The policy, legal and social implications of long-term cohabitation are likely to differ markedly from those flowing from an increase in couples living together for short, essentially childfree, periods. This substantially enhances the value of the present research; and increases the importance of examining the experiences and characteristics of cohabiting mothers.

Background to the research
From our perspective, previous British studies which focused on cohabitation tend to be limited in various ways. These studies either were

based in total upon exceedingly small numbers (for example, Oliver 1982; Chappell 1982) or they included only a small number of cohabiting *mothers* or *parents* (for example, Burgoyne, 1985). Alternatively, such studies are based on secondary analyses, usually by demographers, of large scale datasets or historical documents (for example, Kiernan, 1991; Haskey and Coleman, 1986). Although valuable in their own ways, none of these types of study allows satisfactory investigation of what this research takes to be the critical question, why are increasing numbers of women choosing not to marry when they become mothers? To answer this question, both cohabiting *and non-cohabiting* mothers would need to be interviewed in sufficient numbers so as to allow comparisons between their circumstances and attitudes towards marriage, motherhood and cohabitation. Ideally, both groups of women would be drawn from the same source, and if not wholly representative of cohabiting mothers (from where would one draw such a sample?), they should at least include women in a variety of socio-economic circumstances and from a range geographical regions.

An opportunity to carry out just such a project arose as a result of research conducted in 1988-89 into the operation of British maternity rights legislation. As part of this research, a nationally representative sample of over 7,000 women was drawn from among all women giving birth over a ten-week period in December 1987 and January 1988.[13] Included among the nearly 5,000 respondents to that survey were a number of women who indicated that they were living in the same household with a husband/partner although legally they were either single, divorced or widowed. As access to the original sample had been preserved, it was proposed to carry out interviews with as many of these women as possible, and also to interview a roughly equal number of married respondents to the original maternity rights survey. Funding for the project was made available by the Joseph Rowntree Foundation and, in the late Spring and early summer of 1992, interviews were carried out with some 330 women, who had at least one common characteristic: all were mothers of at least one 4 year old child. More information about research procedures is given in the next chapter, which also describes the outcome of the selection process in relation to the women's current marital status.

Cohabitation in other times
Before proceeding further in the discussion of cohabitation in modern Britain, however, we would wish to place our findings in context. Living together outside marriage is not *something that stopped in ancient Rome to be revived in the 1960s;*[14] nor is it unique to Britain. One historian of marriage estimates that between the mid-eighteenth and mid-nineteenth

centuries as many as one-fifth of the population in England and Wales may have cohabited unlawfully for some period, either as a prelude to legal marriage or as a substitute for it.[15] From the 1750s onward, moreover, rates of unmarried pregnancy and illegitimacy rose to levels unprecedented in recorded British history.[16] From this perspective, it is perhaps the 'rush to marry' which peaked in the 1950s that presents the conundrum, rather than the apparent loosening of the tie between marriage and motherhood that we are witnessing today.

Until the 1750s, marriage in England and Wales was largely a private matter between two individuals and their kin. The Church did not insist upon the posting of banns nor the presence of a priest for the contracting of a valid marriage. Sexual intercourse engaged in after the promise of marriage changed betrothal into marriage.[17] Clandestine weddings carried the same ecclesiastical and civil legitimacy as church weddings, including those conducted by the notorious 'Fleet' clergymen.[18] All this was to change, however, with the passing of the Marriage Act of 1753.

Lord Hardwicke's Marriage Act of 1753, intended 'for the better preventing of clandestine marriages', was an attempt to wreck social custom and to wrest autonomy over marriage from the hands of individuals and vest it in the state. The Act imposed residency requirements on at least one party to the marriage, required parental consent for those aged under 21, the public calling of banns on three occasions or the purchase of a marriage licence,[19] and rendered invalid all marriages other than those performed in a Church of England establishment, a Jewish Synagogue or at a Quaker Meeting.

Parker (1990) sees Lord Hardwicke's act as evidence of the state's wish to *reach down into all aspects of social life to produce a compliant populace*. Gillis (1985) and O'Donovan (1985) consider it testimony to the increasingly successful alliance between property and patriarchy:

> They [the propertied classes] were now convinced that the legality of betrothal together with the church's toleration of clandestine marriage were, as Daniel Defoe was so fond of pointing out, crimes against both property and patriarchy: 'a Gentleman might have the satisfaction of hanging a Thief that stole an old Horse from him, but could have no Justice against a rogue for stealing his Daughter'.[20]

> Formal marriage suited the needs of the upper class for reasons of security of contract, legitimacy of heirs and protection of the rights of property-owners. Publicly and openly celebrated marriage was difficult to deny or to avoid later. Clandestine marriage to unsuitable partners by their children had posed a real threat to the propertied.[21]

It is likely that a variety of reasons and pressures informed the decisions of the legislators who passed Lord Hardwicke's Act. But whatever their intent, one major consequence of the Act is clear, which was to tip large sections of the population into common-law or informal marriage, as ways of living together were sought which suited local and particular interests and preferences rather than the wishes of the state.[22] Or, as Parker put it, Lord Hardwicke's Act introduced a uniform and inflexible definition of marriage which was to trigger in earnest a game of cat and mouse between law and social practice, between governed and government.[23]

Perhaps the best known substitute for official marriage following the imposition of the 1753 Act was the Gretna Green marriage. Because the act applied only to England and Wales, crossing into Scotland and marrying according to the old ways – with the evidenced exchange of consents as the only requirement – became increasingly popular, particularly after the opening up of the Newcastle and Carlisle and the Caledonian railway lines.[24] Parker reports the development of 'package tours' to Gretna Green providing *bed and breakfast service with accommodation both for celebration and consumption.*[25]

More colourful from the vantage point of the late-twentieth century, perhaps, were so-called besom weddings, also known as "jumping the broom". Carried out in front of witnesses, without the intervention of the church, jumping the broom provided an informal way both of marrying and of changing one's mind.

> It was a real wedding in the estimation of the public ... after this manner. A birch besom was placed aslant in the open doorway of a house, with the head of the besom on the doorstone, and the top of the handle on the doorpost. Then the young man jumped over it first into the house, and afterward the young woman in the same way. The jumping was not recognised a marriage if either of the two touched the besom in jumping or, by accident, removed it from its place.[26]

> So let us be married my Mary,
> If ever dislike be our lot,
> We jump'd o'er the broom, then an airy
> jump back shall unfasten the knot.[27]

Gillis reports that it was considered unusual for a besom wedding to fail, but that if this happened, no shame attached to either party and no hindrance existed to further marriages. Fathers would continue to support their children, and women would take with them the personal belongings and wealth which they had brought to the marriage.[28]

'Living tally' was another way in which couples came together in permanent and respectable relationships outside formal marriage. Its origins now obscure, the term, tally, was used widely throughout Britain in the nineteenth century to describe a practice that was distinct from both casual cohabitation and legal marriage.

> They're livin' tally
> They've made a tally bargain
> They're noant wed, they'r nobit livin' tally.[29]

Again, it appears to have been unusual for tally marriages to fail. According to Gillis, couples who lived in open cohabitation were careful to behave in ways that were loving, circumspect and conventional. Indeed, he suggests that their success in doing so and in gaining the approval of family and community provides the explanation for why so little is known about tally couples.[30]

'Jumping the broom' and 'living tally' are but two of what appears to have been a veritable cornucopia of informal marriage practices.[31] What makes their disregard for formal marriage law during the late eighteenth and early nineteenth centuries particularly noteworthy is that the men and women who defied both church and state in this manner were not, as in earlier centuries, vagabonds, ne'er-do-well nor the disinherited. Rather, common-law practices were found throughout Britain, in whole communities, rural and urban, and often where small farming mixed with new manufacturing. Moreover, a fixed certainty of the righteousness of such practices typified the views of many a marital non-conformist:

> The folk of Framlingham say that none but Whores and Blackguards Marry; Honest Folk take each other's words for it.[32]

There were of course many reasons why people might have wished to live together outside formal marriage. Religious dissenters, the poor, under-age lovers, bigamists, recent widows or those with a jointure, all could have provided reasons for not abiding by Lord Hardwicke's Act, as could have men and women who felt that neither state nor church had any business with their private lives.

Another reason for avoiding formal marriage appears directly relevant to the present report: the wish of women to retain personal and financial autonomy. For the most part, the history of marriage is the history of the removal from women of their civil and property rights. O'Donovan suggests that women apparently believed that common-law marriage would preserve their legal rights while giving them respectability within their communities. She notes that some common-law marriages enabled women to retain their names, property, children and places of settlement – all of which would have been lost through formal marriage.[33]

> For women who wished to keep a separate identity, common law rites were extremely attractive. Conventional wedding endangered a woman's access to trade, and Mary Vinson, a London chimneysweep with her own business, was well aware of this when she placed an announcement in the newspaper in 1787: 'Many in the same Business

have reported that I am married again, which is totally false and without Foundation, it being calculated to mislead my Customers.'[34]

We have already noted that at the ending of a besom wedding, women would take back into their possession their own property and dowry. Gillis also reports that it was common for such women to retain their own surnames, and for children to take the names of their mothers.[35] A similar practice recorded by Parker achieved the same end of enabling women to retain their legal and property rights. The 'smock wedding' entailed women to marry wearing only a smock to cover their nakedness, in the belief that, subsequently, their financial obligations and assets would remain separate from those of their husbands.[36]

Furthermore, deliberately 'unmarried' women and their children might be better off in relation to nineteenth century 'social security' should their husbands desert or be taken into the workhouse. Olive Anderson suggests that it was wiser for a woman to engage in a 'little wedding' which was recognised as a proper wedding by her class and community and which preserved her right of settlement, against the possibility of the marriage going wrong. When legally married, a woman's right of settlement was transferred from her own to her husband's parish. Should her husband desert, the wife's original parish could disclaim responsibility for her welfare and her husband's parish often attempted to do the same.[37] As Parker notes, retaining settlement with her own parish might be a better insurance policy for a woman than a formal marriage certificate – an outcome that did not escape the notice of the Royal Commission on the Poor Law:

> These marriages satisfy the conscience of the wife, and while no relief is required of the parish, their invalidity is unknown or unattended to. But as soon as the man becomes chargeable and the parish proceeds to remove him and his family, he shows that he is not legally married, and his children claim settlement on the parishes in which they were born.[38]

Today, informal marriage practices make for colourful and sometimes amusing reading. Taken in their own time and place, however, they provide evidence of the lengths to which ordinary people will go to create lives that make sense, that suit their own preferences and circumstances, rather than those of church and state. Without wishing to suggest that modern cohabitees are in any way the linear descendants of eighteenth and nineteenth century informal spouses, it nevertheless seems clear that we might do well to remember these earlier men and women when exploring modern-day cohabitation. At the very least, recognition that the private ordering of family relationships is likely to have always existed alongside the public ordering[39] may provide a salutary lesson for those who view today's cohabiting mothers as having fallen somehow from a 1950s paradise of wedded bliss into disorder.

Indeed, it may be the single-earner, high fertility family of the 1950s – against which both lone parents and cohabiting couples often are measured and found wanting – which is at odds with history.[40] Largely the product of industrial capitalism, aided by state policies aimed at shifting the economic burden for women and children more firmly onto the shoulders of men,[41] the 1950s family pattern represented the peak of a 'rush to marry' that was well underway by the mid-Victorian period. By 1900, the link between motherhood and marriage had become securely established and the turn of the century witnessed a mass return to legal marriage. People not only married more conventionally, they married at successively younger ages. From 1910 onward, age at marriage declined steadily until the 1950s, when British couples married more often and younger, and had more children and faster, than in any previous, or subsequent, period.[42]

A partial explanation at least for the tightening and subsequent loosening (after the 1960s) of the formal marriage bond seems likely to be found in the pattern of women's labour force participation over the period. It is widely recognised that the development of industrial capitalism undermined the family economy, fixed men firmly into the market economy and foreclosed women's opportunities outside the home. Labour force participation rates of women declined in the late nineteenth century, remained constant until the Second World War and began to rise rapidly in the 1960s. At the turn of the century, fewer than 1 in 10 *married* women worked outside the home. By the 1950s their participation had grown to 1 in 5, only to double again by the 1970s. In 1992, nearly 3 out of 4 women *with dependent children* were in the paid labour force.[43]

For women in the nineteenth and early twentieth centuries, marriage was the main – and for some, the only, avenue to adult status and responsibility.

> With marriage, women assumed their full adult status. ... If marriage was thus an 'important crisis' is a man's life, it could be the key to a woman's future. With the closing of respectable means of earning their own livelihood, some women felt forced into marriage by circumstances, unwilling to remain a burden on their families.[44]

Today, marriage remains an important route to adult status for women (and, of course, for men). But it is also true that women have opportunities for employment undreamt of by their counterparts in the 1850s or, perhaps, the 1950s. Independent living is within the grasp of most women today, albeit at a standard often well below that achievable by employed men. The state continues to seek to shift financial responsibility for women and children on to the shoulders of men,[45] but women without jobs and/or with sole responsibility for children generally are able to remain unmarried if they wish to do so.

Nonetheless, the attraction remains strong to move from being 'someone's child' to becoming 'someone's wife' (husband), and is, as Gittens notes, an important factor in the decision to marry.[46] Increases in cohabitation do not necessarily detract from or challenge this goal,[47] but may instead mark a revival of what Parker calls the private ordering of marriage, or social marriage.[48] Modern-day cohabitation, in other words, may be reflecting the further attenuation of social norms which in the past enforced officially sanctioned ways of living. A society without such norms is likely to face a variety of problems; but it may nonetheless be better placed to allow individual men and women opportunities to define for themselves appropriate ways of living.

And in other places

Of course, neither cohabitation nor its reappearance in recent decades is unique to Britain. Across Western and Northern Europe, as well as in both the United States and Canada, rates of cohabitation have grown markedly. Kiernan and Estaugh (1993) identify three main groupings of countries: those where cohabitation has been well-established for some years; those where it is still emerging as a significant pattern; and those where it remains relatively unknown. Britain, with about 1 in 12 cohabiting couples in 1989, falls into the middle range of European countries, alongside West Germany, the Netherlands, France, Finland, Norway, Austria and Switzerland.[49]

Estimates for West Germany suggest that about 10 per cent of couples were living together in 1986. After three years of cohabitation, 60 per cent had married, 10 per cent had separated and 30 per cent continued to cohabit. Almost half of West Germany's 18-25 year old women were cohabiting in 1988, however; a rise from 1 in 5 of this age group in 1978.

Among households with two adults living together with or without children in The Netherlands, 5 per cent were unmarried couples in 1985. Research conducted in 1984 suggested than 30 per cent of women aged 23-27 had cohabited at some time; among 33-37 year olds, 70 per cent of formerly cohabiting couples had married. In 1986, 59 per cent of 16-19 year old women were cohabiting. Cohabitation in The Netherlands normally lasts no more than 3 or 4 years, and is linked to a rise in the age of marriage.

A recent survey in France indicated that 1 couple in 7 among the population aged 21-44 years was unmarried. The average period of cohabitation prior to marriage was about 22 months; but over time, fewer cohabiting couples appear to be marrying. Among Parisians, cohabitation is increasing viewed as substitute for marriage. Between 1981 and 1986, the proportion of 21-24 year old women living in a cohabiting union more than doubled, from 16 per cent to 36 per cent.

Cohabitation remains relatively rare in the Southern European countries of Italy, Spain, Portugal and Greece, and in Ireland. There are no statistics available about cohabitation in Spain, but reports suggest that it was 'marginal' in 1981 and 'of very little importance' in 1986. Cohabiting Spanish couples are more likely to be found in Barcelona and Madrid, particularly among certain groups of young people, such as artists and students.

Like Spain, there is no statistical information available on the number of cohabiting couples in Ireland. It appears that cohabitation is relatively rare among younger people because of religious pressure and housing shortages. However, a relatively high percentage of separated people reportedly cohabit since divorce (and hence remarriage) remains illegal.

Estimates in Italy suggest that in 1987 just over 1 per cent of all couples were cohabiting, rising to 5 per cent in northern Italy and falling to less than half of 1 per cent in the south where cohabitation is considered socially deviant.

But it is, of course, Sweden and Denmark that have the highest rates of cohabitation in Europe. Kiernan and Estaugh note that although cohabitation was not unknown in parts of Scandinavia before 1960, during the sixties it became more prevalent and visible. In Denmark, it is estimated that 50 per cent of couples live in consensual unions; and that 89 per cent of young people have cohabited at some time. In Sweden, cohabitation is regarded legally and culturally as an accepted alternative to marriage, rather than as a transitional or temporary arrangement. This is reflected in the increasing length of time that couples remain unmarried and in the growing number of couples who never marry at all.[50]

Moreover, having children no longer precipitates marriage between cohabiting Swedish parents. The expectation or birth of a first or second child has only a marginal impact on the chances that a couple will marry.[51] The rapidly declining influence of childbirth on marriage is mirrored in the sharp climb in the percentage of children born to unmarried mothers. In contrast to the 1950s when about 1 in 10 births in Sweden were to unmarried parents, by the late 1980s the proportion had risen to about 1 in 2 births.[52]

But despite having the appearance of equivalent institutions, Swedish cohabiting unions and Swedish marriages do not have the same durability. A study of the dissolution rate of 4,000 cohabiting couples with one child found that on average cohabiting couples were three times more likely to end their union than comparable married couples.[53] The gap in dissolution rates between married and cohabiting couples was narrower for younger couples than for older ones and has probably declined further as the proportion of cohabiting couples has increased. It nevertheless appears that cohabiting unions are more prone to instability and dissolution.[54]

Further studies of unmarried couples who live together have been carried out in the United States. The number of cohabiting households in the United States increased gradually during the 1960s, only to triple between 1970 and 1980. About 4 per cent of couples in the US lived in consensual unions in 1981. Studies carried out during the 1970s showed that unlike many of their Swedish counterparts, unmarried American couples did not consider their cohabitation courtship process to be an alternative to marriage, but saw it as part of the courtship process.[55] Such couples were found to be less traditional than married couples in their attitudes towards gender roles[56] but not very different in the actual division of household labour between partners.[57]

Similar findings have been reported for Australian cohabiting couples. In 1982, almost 5 per cent of couples in Australia lived together without being married.[58] A national survey of 18-34 year olds found that for the majority, cohabitation was a temporary arrangement until the couple felt financially secure enough to marry. Australian cohabiting unions were found to have high termination rates, with marriage remaining the preferred lifestyle.[59] One study found that cohabiting Australian couples were less traditional in the division of household tasks between partners than were married couples.[60]

Studies of cohabitation in other times and in other countries can be instructive through the questions they raise about cohabitation in modern day Britain. Why do couples with children sometimes choose not to marry? What factors might cause them to marry? Is Britain moving towards the Swedish model, where cohabitation appears to have replaced marriage? Or are British couples closer to American or Australian couples in considering cohabitation to be a prelude to marriage? Are cohabiting couples in Britain less traditional than married couples – in behaviour as well as in attitude? Are they happier? These questions, and others, are addressed in the pages that follow.

Notes

1. John R Gillis, *For Better, For Worse: British Marriages, 1600 to the Present*, Oxford University Press, 1985, p.304.
2. Population Trends, 1991.
3. John Ermisch, *Fewer Babies, Longer Lives*, York: Joseph Rowntree Memorial Trust, 1990.
4. Joan Brown, *Why don't they go to work? Mothers on benefit*, Social Security Advisory Committee, HMSO, 1989; Population Trends, 1991.

5. Kathleen Kiernan and Malcolm Wicks, *Family change and future policy*, York: Joseph Rowntree Memorial Trust in association with the Family Policy Studies Centre, June 1990.
6. Kathleen Kiernan, 'Changing marriage patterns', *Journal of Social Work Practice*, Vol 5, No 2, 1991, p.125.
7. Social Trends, 1991:39.
8. Kiernan, op.cit., 1991, p.125.
9. Social Trends, 1991:39.
10. John Haskey and Sue Kelly, 'Population estimates by cohabitation and legal marital status – a trial of new estimates', *Population Trends*, 60, Winter 1991:30.
11. John Haskey and K Kiernan, 'Cohabitation in Great Britain – characteristics and estimated numbers of cohabiting partners', *Population Trends*, 58, Winter 1989, p.25; Kiernan, op.cit., 1991, p.123.
12. Haskey and Kiernan op.cit., 1989, p.24.
13. The Maternity Rights Survey was funded jointly by the Departments of Employment and Social Security and the Equal Opportunities Commission. For more information about the survey, see Susan McRae, *Maternity Rights in Britain: The experience of women and employers*, London: Policy Studies Institute, 1991.
14. Stephen Parker, *Informal Marriage, Cohabitation and the Law, 1750-1989*, Macmillan, 1990, p.161.
15. Gillis, op.cit., 1985, p.219.
16. Ibid., p.110.
17. Katherine Donovan, *Sexual Divisions in Law*, London: Weidenfeld and Nicolson, 1985, pp.42-3.
18. Gillis, op.cit., pp.95-8, p.140; Parker, op.cit., pp.37-8. Parker's discussion includes a quote from Smollett which captures the essence of a Fleet wedding:
    ... a band of profligate miscreants, the refuse of the clergy, dead to every sentiment of virtue, abandoned to all sense of decency and decorum, for the most part prisoners for debt or delinquency, and indeed the very outcasts of human society, who hovered about the verge of the Fleet-prison to intercept customers, plying like porters for employment, performed the ceremony of marriage without licence or question, in cellars, garrets, or alehouses, to the scandal of religion, and the disgrace of that order which they professed. (Smollett, 1830, p.100).
    Parker goes on (1990:38) to tell the story of one of the more successful of these miscreants who was said to marry an average 6,000 couples every year!
19. According to Gillis, the cost of a marriage licence tended to limit its use to the gentry and urban middle classes. By the mid-Victorian period, its cost had risen to 4 guineas; nearly four times the cost of marriage by banns and equivalent to a month's wages for a skilled worker. Gillis, op.cit., p.192.
20. Gillis, op.cit., p.140. The quote from Defoe is from Christopher Lasch, 'The Suppression of Clandestine Marriage in England: The Marriage Act of 1753', *Salmagundi*, No. 26 (Spring 1974), pp.60-109.
21. Donovan, op.cit., p.45.
22. Louise Tilly and Joan Scott, *Women, Work and Family*, New York: Holt, Rhinehart and Winston: 1978, p.97; Gillis, op.cit., p.196.
23. Parker, op.cit., p.47.
24. Olive Anderson, 'The Incidence of Civil Marriage in Victorian England and Wales', *Past and Present*, Vol 69, No.50, pp.67-68.

25. Parker, op.cit., p.64.
26. William Rhys Jones, 'A Besom Wedding in the Ceiriog Valley', *Folklore*, XXXIX (1928) pp.153-54, quoted in Gillis, op.cit., p.198.
27. Nineteenth century song quoted in S.P. Menefee, *Wives for Sale*, Oxford: Blackwell Books, 1981, p.21.
28. From W.R. Jones, 'Lore of Courtship and Marriage', Jones MSS 236, fol. 96, in Gillis, op.cit., p.199.
29. W.R. Jones, 'Living Tally', MS 259/24, Welsh Folk Museum. Quoted in Gillis, op.cit., p.206.
30. Gillis, op.cit., 1985, p.209.
31. Readers who are interested in this area might wish also to see W.J. Fielding, *Strange Customs of Courtship and Marriage*, London: Souvenir Press, 1961; R.B. Outhwaite, *Marriage and Society: Studies in the Social History of Marriage*, London: Europa, 1980; also Parker, op.cit., esp. Chapters 2 and 4.
32. Quoted in Gillis, op.cit., p.209.
33. O'Donovan, op.cit., p.47.
34. I. Pinchbeck, *Women Workers and Industrial Revolution*, Virago, 1981. Quoted in O'Donovan, op.cit., p.47.
35. Gillis, op.cit., p.199.
36. Parker, op.cit., p.28.
37. Anderson, op.cit., p.52.
38. The Report of The Royal Commission on the Poor Law (1834, p.99) quoted in Parker, op.cit., p.69.
40. Andrew Cherlin, 'Changing Family and Household: Contemporary Lessons from Historical Research', *American Sociological Review*, 9. 1983, p.64.
41. During World War I, for example, common-law wives and unmarried mothers were denied government benefits which were extended to the wives and dependents of married servicemen. According to Gillis, this policy contributed to the sharp increase in marriage rates; as had the bastardy provisions of the New Poor Law in 1834. Gillis, op.cit., pp.327-9.
42. Gillis, op.cit., p.232; also Cherlin, op.cit., pp.58-60 for a discussion of the distinctiveness of families in the 1950s.
43. George Joseph, *Women at Work*, London: Philip Allen, 1983, Table B, pp.126-27; 'Women and the labour market: results from the 1991 Labour Force Survey', *Employment Gazette*, September 1992, Table 6, corrected October 1992.
44. Leonore Davidoff and Catherine Hall, *Family Fortunes: Men and Women of the English Middle Class 1780-1850*, Hutchinson, 1987, pp.322-25.
45. April 1993, for example, saw the introduction of the Child Support Agency, which took over responsibility from the courts for the assessment, collection and enforcement of child support maintenance. Anyone who has the care of a child or children and at least one of the parents lives elsewhere in the UK can apply to the Agency for a maintenance assessment. Under the new legislation, women are required to name the father of their children or forfeit a proportion of their benefits. The legislation intends that allowance will be made for women who fear reprisals from their former partners.
46. Diana Gittens, *The Family in Question: Changing Households and Familiar Ideologies, 2nd Edition*, Macmillan, 1993, p.86.

47. Particularly if we interpret getting married as becoming a part of an adult community of couples. cf Gittens, op.cit., p.84.
48. Parker, op.cit., p.4.
49. Information for Europe of the European Community comes from *Families and Policies: Trends and Developments in 1988-89, Final Report.* European Observatory on Family Policies, 1990; and from K. Kiernan and V. Estaugh, *Cohabitation Extra-Marital Childbearing and Social Policy,* Family Policy Studies Centre, 1993.
50. David Popenoe, 'Beyond the Nuclear Family: A statistical portrait of the changing family in Sweden', *Journal of Marriage and the Family*, 49, February 1987, pp.173-83.
51. Britta Hoem, 'One child is not enough: What has happened to Swedish women with one child born in 1936-60?', *Stockholm Research Reports in Demography*, No. 25, Stockholm: University of Stockholm, 1985.
52. Agell, Anders, *Cohabitation without Marriage*, Stockholm: Liber, 1985. (quoted in Popenoe, op.cit.)
53. Hoem, op.cit. 1985.
54. Popenhoe, op.cit., 1987.
55. D. Bower, and V. Christopherson, 'University student cohabitation: a regional comparison of selected attitudes and behaviour', *Journal of Marriage and the Family*, 39, 1977: 447-53; R. Clayton and H. Voss, 'Shacking up: Cohabitation in the 1970s', *Journal of Marriage and the Family*, 39, 1977: 273-83.
56. B. Risman, C.T. Hill, Z. Rubin and L.A. Peplau, 'Living together in college: implications for courtship', *Journal of Marriage and the Family,* 43, 1981: 77-83.
57. R. Stafford, E. Blackman, and P. Dibona, 'The division of labor among cohabiting and married couples, *Journal of Marriage and the Family*, 39, 1977:43-57.
58. S-E. Khoo, 'Living Together as Married: A profile of de facto couples in Australia', *Journal of Marriage and the Family*, 49, 1987: 185-91.
59. S. Sarantakos, *Living together* in Australia, Melbourne: Longman Chesire, 1984, p.59.
60. J.D. Cunningham, and J.K. Anthill, 'Cohabitation: Marriage of the Future', Paper presented at the ANZAAS Congress, Aukland, NZ, 1979. (Quoted in Khoo, op.cit. 1987).

2   Studying cohabiting mothers

Cohabiting mothers rarely have been the focus of research. Reporting the results of interviews carried out in 1979 with 7 cohabiting couples, Oliver (1982) suggests that is it hardly surprising that there is a lack of research designed to explore the reasons why people choose to live together rather than to marry, and cites three problems which await prospective researchers.[1] The first of these is how to define couples who live together: at what point could they be said to be cohabiting – one week, one month, six months? Is it necessary that they have a sexual relationship? What about flat-sharers? Should the analysis be confined only to couples with children?

Solving definitional problems in one way or another gives rise to the second difficulty cited by Oliver: obtaining a representative sample. As she points out, neither the electoral role nor the local taxation register (ratings, poll tax, council tax) give the kind of information needed to distinguish cohabiters from the married; and knocking on doors asking for such information could be both unpleasant and fruitless.

Finally, Oliver suggests that settling the first two problems still leaves the researcher with the difficulty of finding the right questions to ask, particularly in relation to eliciting accurate information about why couples have not married. All this, she argues,

> is not to say that empirical research into cohabitation is not possible; it is possible, and very important, but it would require enormous resources.[2]

For this study, we were fortunate in having to hand a fairly straightforward way of coping with problems one and two, albeit while proving Oliver's point about the costs of such research. However, whether or not we found the right questions to ask must, of course, be left to the reader's judgement.[3]

Defining and locating the sample

We embarked on a study of cohabitation (and resolved problems of defining and locating a suitable sample) essentially because of our realisation of two points. First, we potentially had access to a large number of women known to have given birth while unmarried; and, secondly, little, if anything, was known about the reasons behind what was becoming a major social change in women's behaviour: motherhood within a cohabiting partnership.

In autumn 1988, a postal survey of a nationally representative sample of women who had given birth some 8 or 9 months earlier was carried out in order to assess the operation of British maternity rights legislation. Respondents to that survey had been selected randomly from Department of Social Security (DSS) child benefit records. The DSS was one of the sponsors of the maternity rights research, and kindly agreed to maintain their files in a way which would facilitate access to the survey respondents for future research projects.

Analysis of the maternity rights survey of mothers revealed about 350 women who appeared to be living in consensual unions; that is, they reported that they were either single, divorced, separated or widowed but that they were living with a 'husband/partner'. These women accounted for about 7 per cent of the full survey of mothers (see Appendix 1 for further details). Using them to investigate cohabitation, it was argued, would side-step problems of definition in relation to who counts as a cohabiting couple. It seemed self-evident that men and women who lived in the same household with one or more children were *living together* in the way that this term in commonly used when comparing cohabitation with marriage.[4] Moreover, although we thought (erroneously as it turned out) that a focus on cohabiting women with children would bypass women with other experiences of cohabitation, we considered that a small price to pay for gaining access to such a key group of informants.

Our focus on cohabiting mothers automatically provided us with a sample. However, it was not a representative sample. Although the original survey of mothers had been randomly selected and was therefore representative of women having babies in 1988, the same could not be said about our group of *cohabiting* mothers. To partially offset this unavoidable problem, we decided to select and interview a roughly equal number of married mothers from the same source, matched with the cohabiting mothers by age, education and geographical location.

Fieldwork for the study was carried out in the late spring and early summer of 1992. Participation in interviews was wholly voluntary. Through procedures designed to protect the confidentiality of DSS child benefit records, potential respondents were sent a short, preliminary questionnaire requesting details of their employment, marital status and children, together with a copy of the press release about the original maternity rights survey and a letter requesting their participation in further research.[5] Women who agreed to be interviewed were asked to return the questionnaire, indicating their name, address and telephone number.

Table 2.1 Fieldwork results, cohabiting mothers

	Number	%
Available from 1988 Survey	338	
Removed by DSS	8	
Preliminary questionnaires sent	330	(100)
Returned with name/address	174	(53)
Returned without name/address	62	(19)

By following up the mothers twice, through reminder notices and a new preliminary questionnaire schedule, we expected to gain agreement to be interviewed from about 200-225 women in each group of cohabiting and married mothers. We based this estimate on the work of colleagues who had recently used similar techniques preparatory to a study of low income families, also drawn from DSS child benefit records. The first stage of that research achieved a 62 per cent response rate to the preliminary 'sift' questionnaire. On the grounds that our respondents had indicated their willingness once before to participate in research with PSI, we expected to show a modest increase on these results. In the event, however, we achieved a higher rate of return than expected, but also a high rate of return without names and addresses for further contact.

The results of our fieldwork are shown in Table 2.1, which indicates that overall a 72 per cent response rate was achieved among mothers known to be cohabiting in 1988. Only 53 per cent of cohabiting mothers provided their names and addresses, however. Preliminary questionnaires also were received from 377 married mothers, representing an 80 per cent response. Again, just over 50 per cent provided contact names and addresses. Accordingly, we were able to issue for interviews only 339 names, comprising 174 cohabiting mothers and 165 married mothers. Inteviews were achieved subsequently with 166 'cohabiting' and 162 'married' mothers.

There were no major differences between participants and non-participants in the study, whether previously married or cohabiting. Women designated 'cohabiting mothers' from the 1988 survey who participated in this study were slightly younger than non-participating 'cohabiting mothers'. In addition, they were more likely to have been married and divorced, to have no qualifications, and to have had a father employed in non-manual work. But with the exception of family background, differences between the two groups of 'cohabiting mothers' were not significant. There were virtually no differences in the characteristics of participating and non-participating 'married mothers'. (See Tables A1.2 and A1.3 in Appendix 1 for further details).

A major drawback of our use of the 1988 PSI survey of mothers as the source of cohabiting mothers was the high cost of the fieldwork. The 1988 survey was a postal survey, designed to be nationally representative of women giving birth. As a result, the women we contacted for interviews were scattered throughout England, Scotland and Wales. Interviews took place in locations as far afield as Wick in Scotland and Dawlish in Devon. This inevitably increased the cost of the fieldwork. However, it was felt that the quality and depth of information that could be gained through personal interviewing techniques warranted the extra costs involved in contacting such an unusual group of women.

Interviews were carried out by an agency, in the homes of the respondents. Interviewers worked to a structured questionnaire schedule which included a number of open-ended questions. In addition, respondents were asked to answer questions in a self-completion schedule at differing times in the interview, which generally lasted about 1 hour. The questionnaires are reproduced in Appendix 3.

The outcome of the selection process

Our study of cohabiting mothers derived, then, from research projects which intervened in women's lives at two points: the first in 1988 shortly after they had given birth, and the second some 4 years later. Mothers were selected for inclusion in the *second* project on the basis of their marital status (married or cohabiting) during the *first* project. Moreover, when we began the second project in early 1992, we thought about our respondents in terms of this dichotomy: they had been, four years earlier, either married mothers or cohabiting mothers.

Once we began to analyse the interview data, however, we soon realised that a dichotomy insufficiently described, first, the changes that had occurred *since* 1988 and, secondly, the circumstances that had existed *before* 1988. In particular, we realised that our research was about a dynamic process: a passing of life events which, speaking generally, different women experienced at different times and in different ways. The life events were ordinary ones: establishing an adult relationship and a separate household (cohabiting, marrying), becoming a parent. The timings and ways were highly varied, however; and it quickly became the task of the research to explore, not just why some women have children while cohabiting, but why other women who also cohabit marry before becoming mothers and still other women do not cohabit at all.

The research moved away, then, from a straightforward examination of potential differences between two groups of women – cohabiting mothers and married mothers. In place of this, we adopted an approach which first re-categorised the original two groups of women into eight groups, defined by their experience of cohabitation and the relationship between cohabitation, marriage and motherhood, and taking into account their current (1992) living arrangements. Three groups were subsequently excluded on the grounds of size, leaving 4 primary analytical groups and 1 secondary group.

The first step in this process divided the women into two groups according to whether or not they had ever cohabited, either before *marriage* or before the birth of the four year old child which precipitated their inclusion in the maternity rights survey. These two 'new' groups overlapped with the original 'sample selection' groups, but were not identical to them. Two hundred and twenty-eight women fell into the first group, women who had cohabited either before marriage or in place of marriage; and 100 women who had not lived with their husbands before marrying fell into the second group. When the relationship between cohabitation, marriage and motherhood and current living arrangements was taken into account, 8 separate groups could be constituted. To ease understanding, these various groups are presented diagramatically, in Figure 1 (page 20).

On the far right of figure 1 are found women who did not live with their husbands before marriage. Selected from the maternity rights survey as representative of married mothers, all of this group of non-cohabiting women had married before giving birth.[6] After the exclusion of 8 non-cohabiting women whose marriages had broken down by the time of the interviews in June-July 1992, they formed one of the primary groups used in analyses throughout the report.

The women included in Figure 1 under the heading, 'Got married before motherhood' were also selected from the maternity rights survey as representative of 'married mothers'. After they were interviewed for the second (current) project, we learned that they had cohabited with their husbands before marriage but that they had married before the birth of *any* children, not just before the birth of their four year old child. After the exclusion of 5 women whose marriages had broken down by the time of the second research project, they formed a second primary group for analysis.

The women on the far left of Figure 1 comprise the 'cohabiting mothers' from the maternity rights survey who agreed to take part in a personal interview. Four years before interviewing, all of these women had had a baby while living with a partner. By the time of the interviews, 57 women

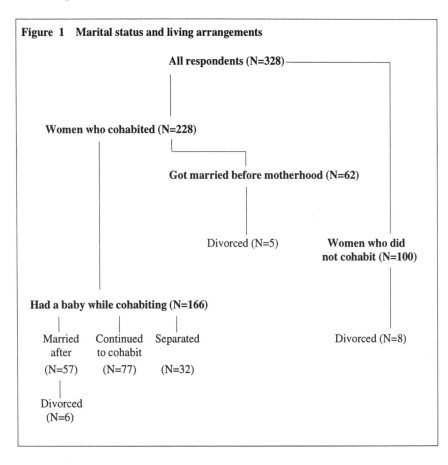

Figure 1   Marital status and living arrangements

had married their partners (and 6 had subsequently divorced), 77 women continued to cohabit with the same partner (that is, with the father of their four year old child) and 32 women had separated from their partners. The first two groups of women make up the remaining two primary analytical groups used in the chapters which follow (after excluding the 6 women who first married and then divorced) bringing the total number of major groups to 4.

We would wish to note here the relatively arbitrary sizes of the group of women who were *continuing* to cohabit (N=77) and the group who had married *after* having children (N=51), which were determined largely by the timing of our research. We show in Chapter 5 that there appears to be a steady flow out of cohabiting-motherhood into married-motherhood. Therefore, if we had carried out our interviews one year later, for example, or six months earlier, the numbers included in these two groups would have been different, as more or fewer cohabiting mothers would have married or separated from their partners.

Further, in constructing our 4 primary groups, we excluded 19 women who had separated from or divorced their husbands at some point before the interviews took place. We took this step largely for methodological reasons: such women were too few in number to separate into constituent groups; putting them all into one group might have hidden important differences between them while still yielding too small a group for tabular analyses. However, we retained a certain interest in women whose *cohabiting* relationships had broken down by the time of our fieldwork. We interviewed 32 women in these circumstances, 10 of whom had gone on to form new cohabiting partnerships. A description of their social characteristics and circumstances is included in Chapter 3, while Chapter 7 focuses on the relationship between their 4 year old child and his or her now absent father.

Generally, however, women whose relationships (marital or cohabiting) had broken down were excluded from our detailed analyses. This decision was taken gradually and reluctantly. As our analyses progressed, the project increasingly came to focus on aspects of intact, ongoing relationships and we were concerned that the incorporation of a few, possibly highly unrepresentative, women whose relationships had broken down threatened to deflect the research from its central concerns.

Long-term cohabiting mothers

The mothers we interviewed who were *continuing* to cohabit with their partners outside formal marriage are a distinctive group of women, even among cohabiting women. For most couples, cohabitation lasts a relatively short time, ending either in marriage or breakdown. Most *pre-marital* cohabitations culminate in marriage within about 18 months. Cohabitations that end without the couple marrying last longer, but few survive for the lengths reported by the women in our study.[7]

The mothers we interviewed who were still cohabiting had been living with their partners just short of 8 years on average. And, of course, they were *continuing* to live with their partners. Combined data from the 1988 and 1989 General Household Surveys suggest that only 9 per cent of cohabiting women live with their partners for 10 years or longer: a duration that many of the mothers we interviewed seemed likely to match and exceed.[8]

We stress the distinctiveness of the long-term cohabiting women we interviewed in order to place in context their views and circumstances. When most women elect to marry before becoming mothers, and when most cohabiting women cohabit for relatively short periods of time, researchers are well-advised to point out the singularity of results which largely focus upon women who differ.

Of course, our study does not focus exclusively on long-term cohabiting women; which is one of its strengths. Instead, the views and circumstances of women with differing histories of cohabitation, marriage and motherhood are examined alongside those of long-term cohabiting mothers. Ultimately, however, the aim of the study is to discover how cohabiting mothers who have not yet married might differ from, or resemble, those who have married, as well as those who did not cohabit before marriage.

Are long-term cohabiting mothers the way of the future? Our research does not allow us to answer the question; but insofar as there is a continuing weakening of the prescriptive norms surrounding marriage, motherhood and the lives of women generally, and the number of cohabiting mothers continues to increase, then it is our hope that the research reported here will have helped us to understand at least some of the reasons behind what must be counted as one of the major social changes of the twentieth century.

Notes

1. Dawn Oliver, 'Why Do People Live Together?', *Journal of Social Welfare Law*, 1982, pp.210-22.
2. Ibid, p.211.
3. In her classic study of 'ordinary' families, Bott suggested that *The achievement of the research consists not so much in finding complete answers as in finding interesting questions to ask.* Although it is perhaps easier to frame interesting questions when interviewing 'extra-ordinary' families, the problem is never entirely absent. See Elizabeth Bott, *Family and Social Network*, Tavistock, 1957, p.5.
4. Because our financial resources were not unlimited, we had to choose between interviewing a large number of cohabiting *mothers* or a smaller number of cohabiting *couples*. We opted for the former, in full recognition that the experiences and views of cohabiting *fathers* equally merit investigation.
5. The procedures followed for the distribution of the preliminary questionnaire that was used to gain consent for interviews were the same as those designed for the 1988 PSI maternity rights survey. Code numbered address labels were prepared by the DSS, using in this case the initial maternity rights survey respondent code number. PSI supplied the DSS with stamped, sealed, coded envelopes enclosing coded questionnaire schedules, again using the original code numbers. The DSS attached the addresses and posted the questionnaires, which were subsequently returned by the mothers to PSI. Mailings to the mothers also included a letter from the DSS which stressed that neither completion nor failure to complete would affect entitlement to benefits. A record was kept in PSI of the serial numbers of questionnaires returned by the mothers. These numbers were forwarded to the DSS where the list of names and addresses was updated in preparation for reminder letters and a new questionnaire schedule.

6.   And hence they had all been selected from the maternity rights survey as 'married mothers'. Four of these women had been married before, but none had given birth prior to their second marriage.
7.   Calculations based on General Household Survey data suggest that the median duration of cohabitation for previously unmarried men and women in 1986-87 was less than two years. For divorced men and women, *post-marital* cohabitation lasts slightly longer: in 1987, their median durations were 35 and 37 months respectively. John Haskey and Kathleen Kiernan, op. cit., 1989. By *post-marital* cohabitation we mean couples living together following the marriage breakdown of either one or both partners.
8.   Kiernan and Estaugh, op.cit., 1993.

3   Social and economic characteristics

This chapter draws a social and economic portrait of the women we interviewed. The purpose is to provide contextual background information, particularly about long-term cohabiting mothers and comparative whenever possible, for the more substantive chapters which follow. So far, we have identified one bit of each woman's life history by assigning her to a particular group according to her experience of cohabitation and the relationship between her entry into motherhood and marriage. In addition, we know that all of the women included in the study had at least one 4 year old child, by virtue of their initial participation in a survey of new mothers in 1988. For just about half of these women (48 per cent), that 4 year old was their first child; overall, their first children ranged in age from 4 to 20 years.

There are, however, a host of other characteristics and circumstances, personal, social and economic, examination of which will improve our understanding of long-term cohabiting mothers. This seems a particularly important task, given both the method we used to select cohabiting mothers for study and the distinctive lifestyle these women have adopted. Our examination of these social and economic characteristics focuses on three questions: first, how far the cohabiting mothers we interviewed resembled long-term cohabiting mothers generally and, secondly, whether *never married* cohabiting mothers differed substantially from women who were cohabiting *post-maritally.*[1] Differences among long-term cohabiting mothers according to their previous marital histories are also reported in Appendix 2. Finally, we note any contrasts which emerged between cohabiting and married mothers. The chapter ends with some summary sketches of the main groups of women included in the study.

Table 3.1 summarises a range of personal and economic characteristics and shows, first, a sharp contrast between the circumstances of long-term cohabiting mothers and those of the married women we interviewed; and secondly, the substantially poorer position of women whose cohabitation had ended in breakdown.

Table 3.1   Selected demographic and household characteristics

Column percentages

	Long-term cohabiting mothers	Cohabited pre-maritally		Non-cohab. married mothers	Cohabitation ended
		Married after baby	Married before baby		
Women's average age (years)	31	30	33	33	27
Average no of children	2.1	2.5	2.4	2.6	1.8
Woman married before	23	28	19	4	19
Partner/husband married before	30	43	18	3	n/a
Others live in household*	5	6	5	7	6
Stepchildren in household	5	20	5	1	13
woman's child(ren)	4	11	5	1	9
man's child(ren)	1	8	0	0	-
both	0	1	0	0	3
No qualifications	30	16	26	32	22
Father's job manual	38	37	40	40	61
Household income £12,000 p.a. or less	51	33	36	26	74**
Owner occupiers	60	71	68	77	25
Base:	*77*	*51*	*57*	*92*	*32*

*   In addition to husband/partner and children
**   £6,000 or less

Age

The average age of the groups of women included in our study ranged from 27 years (formerly-cohabiting women) to 33 years (women who did not cohabit before marriage and cohabiting women who married *before* having children). This age profile makes our group of cohabiting women quite distinctive. Across Europe and in Britain, cohabitation tends to be undertaken while young. Kiernan and Estaugh (1993) show, for example, that 10 per cent or fewer women aged 30-34 years in the late 1980s in Britain, Norway, the Netherlands, France and Austria were cohabiting. Moreover, their re-analysis of General Household Survey data indicated that the large majority of cohabitants in Britain were aged under 35 years (73 per cent of women and 67 per cent of men).

However, we are unable to compare directly the age distribution of the *long-term* cohabiting mothers we interviewed with that of cohabiting mothers generally. This is because Kiernan and Estaugh, our primary source of comparative information, restrict their detailed analyses of cohabiting women with children to women aged 20 to 34 years, while our youngest and oldest cohabiting mothers in 1992 were aged 21 and 49, respectively. It is likely that the differing age distribution of our respondents will have consequences for other comparisons with Kiernan and Estaugh.[2]

We may note, however, that among long-term cohabiting mothers, women who had been legally married before living with their current partners – that is, women who were cohabiting *post-maritally* – were slightly older (average age 34 years) than those who had never married (average age 30 years). In addition, it is worth noting that the partners of long-term cohabiting women ranged in age from 21 years to 54 years. One in 8 partners were aged 45 years or older.[3]

Number of children in the household

The women who participated in our study appeared to have more children than British women in general: since 1973 fertility rates in Britain have been below replacement rates, at about 1.8 children per woman. Here, only women whose cohabiting relationships had ended in breakdown matched this rate, and almost three-quarters of these women indicated that they would like to have more children someday. Among women whose cohabitation was continuing, those who were cohabiting *post-maritally* reported an average 2.5 children, while never-married cohabiting mothers reported an average 2.1 children.

Some small part of the apparent higher fertility shown by women in our study was accounted for by the presence of step-children in the household. This was particularly the case among cohabiting women who married *after* becoming mothers, among whom 1 in 5 had step-children living with them. However, when step-children were discounted, all groups of women except those whose cohabitation had broken down, continued to exhibit higher than average fertility.[4]

Previous marital history

Overall, 16 per cent of the women included in our study, and 21 per cent of their husbands or partners, had been married previously. But as Table 3.1 indicates, respondents with some experience of *cohabitation* were much more likely to have had earlier marriages than those who married without first living together. For example, almost 1 in 4 long-term cohabiting mothers reported a previous marriage; as did almost 1 in 3 cohabiting mothers who married *after* having children, and nearly 1 in 2 of their partners. In contrast, previous marriages were reported by only 1 in 25 women who did not live with their husbands before marriage.

Although no precise comparisons can be drawn between the previous marital histories of our respondents and that of long-term cohabiting mothers generally (the information is not readily available), other research suggests that divorced men and women are more likely to cohabit before marriage than the never married, when comparing those marrying for the second time at the same age and from the same birth cohort.[5] Hence, we would expect to find a substantial proportion of previously-married men and women among our study. Moreover, the older age profile of our respondents itself would be likely to be associated with previous marriages.

It is worth pointing out that the highest incidence of previous marriages was found among cohabiting couples who married *after* having children. Twenty-eight per cent of the women in this group, and 43 per cent of their partners, had been married at least once prior to their current marriage. We noted in Chapter 2 that the distinction between cohabiting mothers who were *continuing* to cohabit and those who had married *after* having children was imposed largely by the timing of our research. Chapter 5 shows that there is, in fact, a steady movement from the former group into the latter, often triggered when one partner (or both) became legally free to marry again.

The presence of step-children in the household

Post-marital cohabitation is likely to be associated with the presence of step-children in the household. Thus it was the case that the group of women which included the highest proportion with prior marriages – cohabiting women who married *after* having children – also included the highest proportion of step-children. Overall, one in 5 of these women reported the presence of step-children, predominately children from a personal previous marriage or relationship, but also from their husband's previous marriage (relationship). This rose to almost 1 in 2 when only women who had been married before were taken into account.

In contrast, having been legally married before cohabiting with their current partners did not appear to affect the likelihood that long-term cohabiting mothers would report the presence of step-children in the household. Seven per cent of each group of long-term cohabiting mothers (married before or not) had children from a previous marriage or relationship.

Women who did not live with their husbands before marriage and who only rarely had been married previously, also were unlikely to report the presence of step-children in the household (1 per cent did so).

Family income and housing tenure

Table 3.1 provides information about variations in family income and housing tenure among the women we interviewed. Women whose cohabitation had broken down by the time of our study tended to be living in very poor financial circumstances, dependent largely upon state benefits and living in council or local authority housing. Table 3.1 indicates that 3 in 4 women who were no longer living with their partners had *net* annual incomes of £6,000 or less, while only 1 in 4 owned or were buying their homes.

The lower family income of long-term cohabiting mothers relative to married mothers – fewer than half reported net annual incomes in excess of £12,000 – also was reflected in lower rates of owner occupation. Sixty per cent of women who were *continuing* to cohabit owned or were buying their homes, compared with about 70 per cent of cohabiting women who had married and 77 per cent of women who did not live with their husbands prior to marriage. Never married long-term cohabiting mothers were particularly unlikely to be owner occupiers: only 55 per cent reported that they owned or were buying their homes, compared with 13 out of 18 of those who had been married before.

It is likely that age differences account for some part of the variation in housing tenure among long-term cohabiting mothers, of whom the previously married were on average 4 years older than the never married. The older age profile of long-term cohabiting mothers is likely also to account for differences in housing tenure between our study and the 1989 GHS re-analysis carried out by Kiernan and Estaugh, which was restricted to women aged 20-34 years. Only 39 per cent of cohabiting women with children were shown by Kiernan and Estaugh to be owner occupiers, compared with 60 per cent in this study.

Kiernan's and Estaugh's analyses suggest further that cohabiting couples with children were the poorest group among married and cohabiting couples (with and without children); findings which are clearly in line with our own results. According to Kiernan and Estaugh, 23 per cent of cohabiting couples with children had *gross* weekly household incomes of less than £100 in 1989, compared with 6 per cent of married couples with children. Our own results suggest that 18 per cent of long-term cohabiting couples with children had *net* annual household incomes of less than £6,000 in 1992, compared with 6 per cent of women who married *before* having children (whether or not they cohabited pre-maritally).

Kiernan and Estaugh also show that compared with married couples with children, cohabiting families were much less likely to have telephones or cars, or luxury items such as microwaves, home computers and tumble driers. We did not explore this aspect of family life, but would concur with the general comment of Kiernan and Estaugh that

> On most of the available measures, cohabiting couples with children are less well off than their married counterparts.

Economic activity

A large part of the explanation for the poorer economic circumstances of long-term cohabiting couples is provided in Table 3.2 which summarises household economic activity. Long-term cohabiting mothers were less likely to be in paid work than married women, while their partners were more likely than married men to be unemployed and to be unemployed for longer durations. One in 4 long-term cohabiting families had no paid workers; only 40 per cent had both partners in employment.

These patterns of employment and unemployment reflect the general pattern. This is borne out in a comparison with Kiernan and Estaugh, who show that 43 per cent of cohabiting mothers, but 53 per cent of married mothers, were in paid work in 1989. The 1991 Labour Force Survey similarly shows that cohabiting mothers whose youngest child was aged 4 or younger were less likely than married women to be in paid work, and more likely to be unemployed (38 per cent and 46 per cent, respectively, in paid work; 10 per cent and 5 per cent, respectively, in unemployment). Tables A2.3 and A2.4 in Appendix 2 summarise the reasons given by women for working or for remaining outside the labour force.

A further comparison with Kiernan's and Estaugh's re-analysis of the 1989 GHS suggests that the extent of unemployment among the cohabiting fathers included (by proxy) in our study also reflects the general pattern. One in 5 cohabiting fathers surveyed by the GHS were unemployed, compared with 22 per cent of cohabiting fathers in our study. Moreover, both investigations indicate that all but a handful of cohabiting mothers with unemployed partners were themselves outside the labour force.

Table 3.2   Economic activity

Column percentages

| | Long-term cohabiting mothers | Cohabited pre-maritally | | Non-cohab. married mothers | Cohabitation ended |
		Married after baby	Married before baby		
Woman in paid work	43	57	51	52	40
Partner/husband unemployed	22	10	12	5	n/a
Average duration of unemployment (months)	24.4	16.2	17.2	16.6	n/a
Both partners in work	40	53	49	53	n/a
Neither in work	23	14	11	5	n/a
Base:	*77*	*51*	*57*	*92*	*32*

n/a Not applicable

Social class distribution

Table 3.3 categorises respondents and their partners/husbands into three social classes according to their current job or, for unemployed men, their last job. In addition, the table shows the extent to which the couples included in our study were part of the service class, which comprises large proprietors, managers, professionals and the like.

The most interesting findings in Table 3.3 emerge in the last panel which confirms the generally disadvantaged position of long-term cohabiting couples: in only 8 per cent of such families were both partners employed in service class jobs; in only an additional 22 per cent was at least one partner in a service class job. In each instance, married couples – whatever their history of cohabitation – were more widely represented in service class occupations than cohabiting couples. A particularly sharp contrast is with cohabiting couples who married *before* becoming parents, of whom 26 per cent consisted of both partners in service class jobs.

Table 3.3   Social class distribution

Column percentages

	Long-term cohabiting mothers	Cohabited pre-maritally Married after baby	Married before baby	Non-cohabiting married mothers
Woman's current job				
Service class	39	35	55	33
Intermediate	24	35	28	33
Working class	36	31	17	34
Base:	*33*	*29*	*29*	*49*
Partner's last or current job				
Service class	22	33	44	41
Intermediate	36	33	25	29
Working class	38	26	28	29
No answer	4	8	4	0
Service class				
Both in service class jobs	8	14	26	12
One in service class job; other in work	14	14	0	16
Partner in service class job; woman not in work	8	12	18	18
Base:	*77*	*51*	*57*	*92*

Regional distribution

Table 3.4 summarises the distribution of respondents across the 11 major regions of England, Scotland and Wales, and provides a comparison with the geographical distribution of cohabiting women in 1986-87. Respondents are designated 'cohabiting' or 'married' *according to the status they reported in the 1988 Maternity Rights Survey*. The central column of the table is the pivotal column: it represents the regional distribution of all 'cohabiting' – in 1988 – mothers who returned preliminary questionnaires and with whom interviews were carried out in 1992. 'Married' mothers were selected for interviews on the basis of their geographical proximity to 'cohabiting' mothers (following a matched

Table 3.4   Regional distribution

Column percentages

Region	Cohabiting women 1986-87*	All 'cohabiting' mothers	All 'married' mothers
South East	17	24	25
Greater London	16	8	5
East Anglia	18	4	1
South West	15	8	7
West Midlands	17	11	13
East Midlands	14	5	7
Yorks & Humberside	13	13	13
North West	11	15	10
Northern	13	3	5
Wales	8	4	6
Scotland	10	6	10
Base:		*166*	*162*

*   Proportion of all women aged 16-59 who were cohabiting in 1986/87 (Source: Haskey and Kiernan, 1989).

selection by age and education); the generally similar distribution of the two groups of respondents is therefore the result of the methods we chose to select study participants.

The first column of the table indicates the proportion of cohabiting women among all women aged 16-59 in each region and is based on calculations from the General Household Survey by Haskey and Kiernan (1989). It shows a distinct regional pattern in the distribution of cohabiting women: as one moves further away from south eastern England, the proportion of cohabiting women declines. Women in Greater London, for example, appear to be twice as likely to cohabit as women in Wales; while Scottish women are markedly less likely to do so than their counterparts in East Anglia.

It is not possible, of course, to compare this information directly with the distribution of our initial group of 'cohabiting' mothers because of the different ways that the two sets of figures are presented. Moreover, GHS data refer to all cohabiting women, while our own data relates strictly to cohabiting women with children. Therefore, from Table 3.4 we would wish to note only that the 'cohabiting mothers' initially included in our study,

Table 3.5   Regional distribution, according to marital/cohabitation history

Column percentages

| | Long-term cohabiting mothers | Cohabited pre-maritally | | Non-cohab. married mothers | Cohabitation ended |
		Married after baby	Married before baby		
South East	21	35	37	22	16
Greater London	9	6	9	3	6
East Anglia	4	4	0	1	3
South West	8	2	9	4	13
West Midlands	12	6	9	17	19
East Midlands	8	0	2	8	6
Yorks & Humberside	10	14	9	16	16
North West	13	18	9	11	16
Northern	4	4	4	4	0
Wales	4	4	5	2	3
Scotland	8	4	9	11	3
Base:	*77*	*51*	*57*	*92*	*32*

that is, women who gave birth in 1988 while living in a consensual union, were as likely to live in south eastern England (32 per cent) as they were to live in the north and Scotland (35 per cent).

Table 3.5 summarises the regional distribution of the study participants according to their marital status and living arrangements when interviewed in 1992. A number of comments appear germane. First, mothers who were *continuing* to cohabit were less likely to be living in south eastern England than cohabiting mothers who married either before or after having children. Over 40 per cent of the latter lived in the South East or Greater London, compared with only 30 per cent of long-term cohabiting mothers. Secondly and consequently, long-term cohabiting mothers tended to be fairly evenly distributed across a north-south axis; but it is possible that our study under-reports the experiences of still-cohabiting women in Greater London. Thirdly, women whose cohabitation had broken down by the time of our study were markedly more likely to be found in the Midlands and northern England (57 per cent) than in the south of England, but appeared to be under-represented in Scotland (3 per cent).

Moreover, it is worth noting that among our 'married' respondents, women who did not live with their husbands before marriage were much less likely to live in the south of England or in Wales, and much more likely to be found in northern England (39 per cent) and Scotland (11 per cent). In contrast, the southern concentration of cohabiting women who married *before* becoming mothers was the highest found, with 46 per cent living in the South East and Greater London. One may only speculate here about the reasons for this geographical disparity among married women; and in doing so, it is tempting to think about traditional northern communities exerting greater social and sexual control over women.[6]

There have been many opportunities for women to select themselves out of participating in our research; hence, the regional variations presented above should be taken as little more than indicative.[7] But they are interesting and at times appear to flout expectations about cohabiting women: that is, Greater London was generally under-represented; there were virtually no cohabiting women living in East Anglia; long-term cohabiting women were almost as likely to be found in the north as women who did not live with their husbands before marriage. Cohabiting mothers they may be, but 'trendy Londoners' they are not.

Some brief sketches

As a companion to the detailed analyses which follow in the remaining chapters, some brief, summary sketches of each group of mothers are provided.

Long-term cohabiting mothers

Our group of long-term cohabiting mothers was unevenly composed of single (never married) and formerly-married women. One in 4 had been married before establishing her current relationship. These women tended to be older than never married cohabiting mothers, to have more children and to be more likely to own or be buying their homes. Otherwise, few major differences in social and economic circumstances were identified, but it is important to bear in mind the disparate sizes of the two groups of women, noting particularly that only 18 formerly-married, long-term cohabiting mothers were included in the study.

As a group, long-term cohabiting mothers tended to be living in poor economic circumstances, although a minority appeared to be better off: 1 in 10 reported net family incomes above £24,000 per year. The majority, however, appeared to gain their living primarily from state benefits or poorly paid jobs. One in 2 reported net annual incomes of £12,000 or less.

Long-term cohabiting mothers were unusually likely to be out of the labour force, often because they held traditional views about the roles of women with young children (see Table A2.3). Indeed, the chances were about 1 in 4 that no one in long-term cohabiting households would be in paid employment. Once unemployed, moreover, long-term cohabiting fathers tended to remain out of work for long periods. When interviewed, 1 in 5 cohabiting fathers had been unemployed for just over 2 years on average.

Cohabiting women who married after having children

Cohabiting women who married *after* becoming mothers were distinctive in relation to the fact that their marriages were likely particularly to be second marriages for themselves, their husbands or for both partners. They were found typically in the South of England, in their own houses, where it was likely that there were co-resident step-children.

In addition, cohabiting women who married *after* having children were slightly younger on average than both married women and those who were continuing to cohabit; and were the least likely to have left school without qualifications. When employed, both husband and wife were fairly evenly distributed across the occupational structure, but in 1 in 7 families, neither husband nor wife had paid work. Thus, although 1 in 4 had net family incomes above £24,000 per year, the annual incomes of a further 1 in 3 were £12,000 or less.

Cohabiting women who married before having children

The typical habitat of cohabiting women who married *before* having children was the South East and Greater London, where they were likely to own their homes and to work in service class occupations. Moreover, chances were better than 1 in 4 that both husband and wife were employed in the service class, yielding an annual net income of £18,000 or more for 40 per cent. About 1 in 6 had net annual incomes in excess of £24,000.

However, not all women included in this group were affluent: in 1 in 10 households, neither husband nor wife were in paid work, and almost 1 in 3 had net incomes of £12,000 or less.

Otherwise, cohabiting women who married *before* having children were not particularly distinctive: about 1 in 5 had been married previously; about 1 in 5 of their husbands had been married before.

Non-cohabiting married mothers

Women who did not live with their husbands before marriage were distinctive in the sense of the traditional stability that appeared to be associated with their circumstances. These women were among the oldest respondents, with the largest families, and were the most likely to have left school without qualifications.

Very rarely had either husband or wife been married previously; typically, they lived in their own homes, with the children from their own marriages, and were found much more frequently in the North and Scotland than in the South or Wales.

Women who did not live with their husbands before marriage were the least likely to have an unemployed husband or to live in households were no one was in work. Indeed, chances were better than 1 in 2 that both husband and wife would be in paid work, albeit not necessarily in service class jobs. About 1 in 3 had net annual family incomes of £12,000 or less; for almost 40 per cent, their net annual incomes were £18,000 or above.

Formerly cohabiting women

Women whose cohabiting relationship had ended in breakdown by the time of our study came largely from working-class family backgrounds and were among the youngest women we interviewed, with the smallest number of children. When interviewed, the majority (69 per cent) were lone parents, although 10 women had formed new cohabiting relationships.

Only 40 per cent of formerly cohabiting women were in paid work; among those who had formed new relationships, half lived in households with no one in paid work. Consequently, the large majority (3 out of 4) had net annual incomes of £6,000 or less and lived in council or local authority housing. Problems finding or affording suitable childcare was the largest single deterrent to employment for these women.

Our findings suggest that long-term cohabitation is associated with either low-paid employment or unemployment, and, consequently, with financial hardship; cohabitation breakdown, however, is likely particularly to result in straitened circumstances.

Notes

1. In reporting our findings, we generally treat long-term cohabiting mothers as homogeneous when in fact they include both never-married and previously-married women. In large measure, this approach was adopted because of the limited number of *post-marital* cohabitants in the study (18). But in addition, we felt that to disaggregate 4 already small groups of women (because all groups included previously- and never-married women) into even smaller groups would have radically jeopardized the comparative picture that the report is hoping to create of mothers who taken very differing marital and cohabiting routes. We recognise, however, that differences exist between previously-married and never-married women in many respects. Some of these are touched on in the text. Further information is available in Kiernan and Estaugh, 1993.

2. The modal age of the women included in the survey was 35 years. The age distribution of women respondents to the 1988 PSI Maternity Rights Survey, from which the current study sample was drawn, was skewed towards older mothers: nationally, 37 per cent of women having babies in 1988 were under age 25,

compared with 28 per cent of women who responded to the PSI survey. Bias in the 1988 survey is likely to be reflected in the current study.

3. The median age of the respondents' partners was 34, while the modal age was 35 years.

4. The 1991 GHS reports average family size of 2.1 children for step-families and 1.85 for other families. It may be of interest to note that 1988 in general, and the sample drawn for the Maternity Rights Survey in particular, were notable for the number of multiple births recorded. 1988 had the highest number of multiple births recorded since information was first collected. Seventy-seven of the respondents to the 1988 survey had had multiple births: 65 twins, 7 triplets and 5 sets of quads.

5. John Haskey, *Population Trends*, No 68, Summer 1992.

6. It is important to note that ethnic origin is not a factor here; the study is based overwhelmingly on the experiences of white women.

7. In order to be a part of the current study, women needed to:

1. return the 1988 Maternity Rights Survey questionnaire;

2. maintain a current address with the DSS;

3. return the 1992 preliminary questionnaire, and include their names and addresses;

4. agree to a personal interview when contacted in June/July 1992.

4   Cohabitation or marriage? – cohabitation

A central reason for studying cohabiting mothers was to gain some understanding of the apparent weakening of the link between motherhood and marriage. There is a tendency to treat cohabitation as if it does not differ from marriage in any important respects. This response was apparent in the early 1970s, when very few couples lived together outside marriage. For example, in a highly influential contribution to the study of marriage, Jessie Bernard likened cohabitation to marriage as simply one of many forms through which marital commitment may be manifested.

> ... one fundamental fact underlies the conception of marriage itself. Some kind of commitment must be involved. Without such commitment a marriage may hardly be said to exist at all ... The form of the commitment is less important than the emotional contents it underlines. It may be a written contract or simply vows and promises made before witnesses or even simply an 'understanding' or consensual arrangement.[1]

Twenty years later, when rates of cohabitation have grown to encompass about 1 in every 12 couples, the tendency to treat it as essentially identical to marriage remains. In an expansive review of marriage and the family by Delphy and Leonard, discussion of cohabitation is sparse, while a final comment suggests that *cohabitation is no longer very different from marriage.*[2] Of course, this view may be accurate; but it is based on little empirical evidence either about cohabitation which does not end in marriage or about pre-marital cohabitation. Indeed, what evidence there is suggests that in the past cohabiting and marital relationships have differed in at least one important respect: durability.

Recent demographic analyses have suggested that couples who lived together before marriage were more than twice as likely to experience divorce or separation within 15 years of marriage as couples who did not pre-maritally cohabit. That is, the risk of divorce was found to be significantly greater for marriages preceded by pre-marital cohabitation, even when the start of living in a consensual union was treated as the start of the 'marriage'.[3] However, it is important to note the possibility that couples who began to cohabit in the sixties and seventies (the generations covered by these analyses) are likely to have been fairly unconventional and as such, may have been more prone to marital disruption than other, non-cohabiting couples. Whether the association between pre-marital cohabitation and marriage breakdown will continue to hold when over half of all men and women cohabit for at least some part of their early years remains to be seen.

However, research has shown that important differences exist between the economic circumstances and life chances of women who continue to cohabit long after becoming mothers and those of women who marry. Accordingly, it seems reasonable to assume that other differences between women who marry and those who cohabit may exist which have hitherto been obscured by a lack of primary research.

To begin to uncover such differences, we explored the following issues: What influenced the initial decision of women who had cohabited to set up home together with their partners. Why women who ultimately married chose to cohabit first rather than marry straight away; why they decided to marry. Why women who continued to cohabit had chosen not to marry; and what might influence their decision to marry. What were considered to be the advantages and disadvantages of cohabitation (if any). Whether women who had had a child while cohabiting had ever felt pressure to marry, and if so, from whom.

Of course, the women who participated in our research had differing experiences of cohabitation. For one group of women, cohabitation had not (yet) ended, and these women recorded the longest duration of cohabitation, averaging 7.8 years. Another group of women had never cohabited and had been married, on average, for 11 years. Among women who had cohabited pre-maritally and married their partners *before* becoming mothers, cohabitation had been fairly short-lived, averaging just less than 2 years, and had ended at least 4 years before our research was carried out. Cohabiting women who married their partners *after* becoming mothers had cohabited for just over 4 years on average; and for some, cohabitation had ended only a few months before our interviews. It seemed reasonable at the outset of our analyses to expect that these different histories of cohabitation and marriage would have implications for women's views about their living arrangements – an expectation that is amply confirmed below.

Living together

What reasons do people give for their decisions to set up home together? According to a recent study of men and women in six British cities, the large majority of women in all social groups begin to live together or get married because they are in love (the Social Change and Economic Life

Initiative - SCELI). Having enough money to set up an independent household also enters in, as does being at a suitable point in one's working life; but love appears largely unrivalled, and over three-quarters of SCELI's female respondents gave this as the reason why they had set up home with a partner or married.[4]

The Social Change and Economic Life Initiative (SCELI) was not intended to focus directly on respondents' marital histories and thus did not distinguish between the decision to live together and the decision to marry. Burgoyne (1985) focused exclusively on cohabitation and identified three avenues to living together among her largely middle-class, childless couples. Such couples may undertake to live together as a test of their relationship – a trial marriage. Alternatively, they may live together with little expectation of permanence: the arrangement suits them at the moment. Thirdly, a stable cohabiting relationship may evolve from an earlier, more temporary relationship or from sharing the same accommodation.[5]

All of these reasons for cohabitation find resonance in our own study of cohabiting and married mothers. For cohabiting mothers, however, pregnancy also was a major precipitating factor. Among SCELI's respondents, 1 in 10 women reported that being pregnant influenced their decision to set up home or get married.[6] Among the mothers we interviewed who were *continuing* to cohabit, however, the proportion was 1 in 5 – rising to 1 in 2 among mothers whose cohabitation *after* the birth of a baby had culminated in marriage. These figures are shown in Table 4.1, which summarises the range of factors which influenced the point in life when *cohabiting* women first set up home with their partners.[7]

Apart from pregnancy, few differences separated the three groups of women shown in Table 4.1.[8] Somewhat surprisingly, perhaps, the only other major difference concerned the extent to which falling in love figured as a response. For two-thirds of women who cohabited but married *before* giving birth, cohabitation had been triggered by falling in love; for the other two groups, pregnancy and the desire for a regular sexual partner had been as important as falling in love.[9] It seems reasonable to suggest that, in the absence of pregnancy, falling in love represents the spontaneous and romantic ideal which is supposed to govern all our lives and lead us to becoming part of a couple. After all, if you were not pregnant, why else would you have lived with the man you ultimately married?[10]

Table 4.1 also shows the influence of housing on the decision to establish a cohabiting relationship. Housing availability may have a marked influence on the decisions of young couples to establish a home together. A recent Rowntree Foundation study of the effects of housing costs on young people's lifestyles reported that about 1 in 7 18-35 years olds in the

Table 4.1   Factors influencing the decision to cohabit

Column percentages

	Long-term cohabiting mothers	Cohabited pre-maritally	
		Married after baby	Married before baby
Fell in love	51	51	65
Pregnancy	23	49	12
Wanted regular sexual partner	31	33	23
Wanted a child*	13	6	7
Rented accommodation available	21	24	25
Could afford a house	18	18	14
Previous household split up	10	6	14
Couldn't stand previous household	14	12	9
At suitable point in working life	0	2	7
Base:	*77*	*51*	*57*

Notes

*   Excluding those who also indicated that pregnancy was a precipitating factor in their cohabitation decision.

Sums to more than 100 per cent because multiple reasons possible.

South-East had delayed setting up a home with their partners because of the high cost of housing.[11] However, no substantial differences among women in relation to the impact of housing decisions emerged from our analyses. Nor were there any substantial differences in relation to the timing of cohabitation in terms of the women's working lives, although it might fairly be supposed that the slightly greater tendency for women who cohabited but married *before* giving birth to cite a work-related reason reflects their generally higher occupational standing.

But it remains in relation to pregnancy that differences are most pronounced between women who cohabited after giving birth (whether or not they ultimately married) and those who married before giving birth. Women who cohabited *after* giving birth were substantially more likely to establish a household with their partner *because they were pregnant.* Further: their pregnancies were largely unplanned. Unexpected first pregnancies were reported by 71 per cent of mothers who pre-maritally cohabited after a birth and 58 per cent of mothers who continued to cohabit. This contrasts with 32 per cent of women whose pre-marital cohabitation ended before they became mothers and 27 per cent of women who did not cohabit before marriage (and 34 per cent of female SCELI respondents).

Of course, differences existed between mothers who were *continuing* to cohabit and those who married sometime *after* a birth: indeed, twice as many of the latter (49 per cent) as the former (23 per cent) reported that they were pregnant when they first set up home with their partners. This is likely to reflect in part at least the higher proportion of second marriages among women who married after a birth: waiting for a divorce affected the (re)marriage timing of about 1 in 5 of these women. But in addition, it seems that for some of these women, pregnancy was not only a precipitating reason for living with their partners, it was the reason they chose *not* to marry, thus bringing them into our category of cohabiting women who married after giving birth. That is, it was the fact of pregnancy itself that stopped them from marrying – at least until after the baby was born.

Reasons for delaying marriage

Table 4.2 summarises the reasons why cohabiting women who married did not do so straight away but instead lived with their husbands for a period. [12] Almost 1 in 5 (18 per cent) of those who had had a baby *before* they married reported that they had not married because they were pregnant:

> We thought it better to wait till our son was born. I didn't want to get married when I was all fat. 201/1460

> At the time I was expecting a baby and I didn't want to get married when I was pregnant, I preferred to wait. I would say basically because [then it would have seemed as if] I was pressurised into it, so I thought it was better to wait. 075/5535

> I wanted everyone to celebrate our marriage because we were in love and not because I was pregnant. I felt it would have spoilt the day and it was the wrong reason to get married at that time. 091/4263

For these women at least, the idea of a *shotgun wedding* was an anathema: better to wait until their child was born and then consider getting married. Indeed, more than one woman suggested that they had no wish to give hostages to fortune by appearing to use their pregnancy to force their partners into marriage.

The fact that pregnant women might choose to cohabit rather than to marry is itself one measure of the changes that have occurred in British society since the 1960s. So too is the fact that almost 1 in 5 (18 per cent) of the women who did not marry until after they had become mothers postponed marriage because they or their partners were still legally married to someone else. Research by Haskey shows that pre-marital cohabitation is particularly likely before second marriages: *the prevalence of pre-marital cohabitation before second marriages is always higher than that before first marriages, when comparing those marrying for the second time at the*

Table 4.2   Reasons for pre-marital cohabitation

Column percentages

| | Cohabited pre-maritally | |
	Married after baby	Married before baby
One or both did not want to marry	27	16
Trial marriage	27	25
Waiting for a divorce	18	14
Couldn't afford it	14	14
Didn't want to marry while pregnant	18	0
Other reasons	12	32
Accommodation became available	0	9
Base:	*51*	*57*

Note: Sums to more than 100 per cent because more than one reason possible.

same age and from the same birth cohort.[13] In other words, an important ingredient of the rise in cohabitation is an increase in the rate of divorce and re-marriage. Living together is a way of becoming part of a couple again, of testing the water, without the complications of marriage:

> We had both been married before so we were not in a hurry to get embroiled again – once bitten, twice shy! We got married after our son was born. 204/3407

> Well, we both had been married before and we knew of some of the complications that can happen and we just didn't think it was the time to get married. We thought we would wait and see if things would work out. 188/4794

> [We wanted] to find out whether we could get on together. My husband didn't want to get married again until he was ready, so I waited for him. If you live together you can find out whether you can stand being in the same place as that person. 156/5596

Moreover, as the words of the last woman suggest, there is often more than one reason why a couple postpones marriage:

> It seemed silly having two places and both paying out [rent] for them. We just did not feel the need to get married straight away and also his divorce wasn't through. 121/1389

> We couldn't afford it and never thought about marriage and we had both been married before. That's it really. 240/0327

The preceding two quotations, which come from women who married after a period of cohabitation but *before* becoming mothers, do more than illustrate the multiplicity of influences on women's decisions to marry or not. They show also the common ground between the two groups of women included in Table 4.2. Few large differences were found in the reasons these women offered for not marrying straight away. Women who married *before* becoming mothers were less likely to report that they cohabited because one or the other did not want to marry, and more likely to offer a long, straggling tail of reasons. This accounts for the fact that about one-third of the reasons given by these women fell into an 'other' category. Included here were 2 women who felt they were too young to marry (but not to cohabit), 2 women who wanted to finish their education or training before marrying, 2 who reported problems finding the right time to get married, and 1 who began living with her husband because she had *nowhere else to go*:

> because I was getting physically abused where I was living and we were engaged. I didn't want to go back home and he was moving North and asked me to come with him. We had a date set for getting married when we decided to live together. 137/0564

This long tail of reasons notwithstanding, the explanations given by these two groups of women about why they chose first to cohabit rather than to marry have much in common, with one marked exception: their attitudes towards pre-marital pregnancy. Substantially fewer cohabiting women who married *before* becoming mothers experienced unplanned first pregnancies; but when they did so, their response was to marry:

> The only reason why we got married was because I was pregnant. We were quite happy living together, we had more freedom before marriage. 272/3262

> We loved each other and I was pregnant and we wanted to get married before we had the child. 151/5645

This view was shared also by women who married well before becoming pregnant:

> We both came from divorced parents. Looking back we realised that they got married before they knew each other. We decided to live together and see if we really got on well, and learn to live together. We then felt that we could live happily together and so got married. I would not have had children had I not been married. I don't think it would have been very good for the children, later on, to see on their birth certificates parents with different surnames. I do care about that. 110/2787

Continuing to cohabit

All of the women included in Table 4.2 had married by the time we interviewed them in 1992: their period of cohabitation, in other words, had turned into a period of *pre-marital* cohabitation, and we examine later the reasons why they married. Women who were *continuing* to cohabit when we contacted them also were asked why they had not married. Because we wished to capture the full range of possible responses, our question to long-term cohabiting mothers was unprompted and open-ended.[14] Two points are worth noting, however, before we proceed to an examination of this critical issue.

First, we would emphasise that the views represented in Table 4.3 come from a selection of highly unusual women: those who, by the early 1990s, were long-term cohabiting mothers. Their views may not be representative of all cohabiting mothers; but it seems likely that they signal the types of influences that might encourage increasing numbers of women in the future to become and to remain parents outside of formal marriage.

Secondly, we would note that although our research asked long-term cohabiting mothers why they had chosen not to marry, we recognise that not marrying need not be the outcome of a deliberate or calculated decision. Rather, couples who live together (like married couples) simply may accept the day-to-day contours of their lives and not act to change them. Time passes surprisingly quickly, and unless there are compelling reasons to marry, marriage just might not happen. Of course, this is itself a 'choice', and one with specific (although diminishing) legal and social consequences, as we see below.

Indeed, implicit within the responses of several women was the sense that no decision had been taken about marrying or not marrying. They had simply not married. One woman made her position explicit:

> It isn't a decision we have made not to get married, we have just not made the decision to get married. You don't sit down and first say 'we are not getting married'. Now, having not chosen to not get married, I could not be less interested [in marriage]. 029/2152

These views notwithstanding, most of the long-term cohabiting mothers we interviewed were able, when asked, to provide reasons for not having married. These reasons are summarised in Table 4.3

Avoiding marriage

A wish to avoid the institution of marriage, expressed either as opposition towards marriage or as apathy, was by far the most common reason given for continuing to cohabit over the longer term. Just over half of the long-term cohabiting mothers we interviewed said either that they were

Table 4.3　Reasons why long-term cohabiting mothers have not married

Column percentages

	Long-term cohabiting mothers
Against marriage	21
No advantage in marriage	30
Weddings too expensive	26
Marriage delayed	19
Divorce as deterrent	30
No reason	6
Base:	*77*

Note: Sums to more than 100 per cent because more than one reason possible.

against marriage (21 per cent) or that they could see no advantage in getting married (30 per cent).

> I don't particularly believe in the sanctity of marriage; having seen a lot of married couples and their carryings-on over the years made it seem irrelevant. Neither of us is religious. We did actually get engaged but never followed it through. We're both just happy as we are. 235/2235

> My partner does not really believe in marriage and we have lived so long together, very happily, that the matter has not been important. 221/1694

> I've just got no interest in being married. We live as a couple and we're quite satisfied with the way we are. I've been married and it's no different than living together. 324/4286

Women giving these types of reason had lived with their partners longer than other long-term cohabiting mothers, averaging just over 8 years together. About one-third had no qualifications (although 8 per cent had degrees) and almost half had household incomes of £12,000 or less. They were the most likely of long-term cohabiting mothers to be in paid work (60 per cent), and two-thirds had had an employed mother when they were growing up. Not surprisingly, a desire for personal independence often figured in their decisions not to marry:

> I don't like the institution of marriage. I find it oppressive. It is a prison once you are married. I like living together, it suits my needs and feelings in life. 044/4365

It's my decision rather than my partner's. I feel more independent not being married. I do not feel tied but am here by choice in this relationship. 206/1494

The cost of weddings

Costly, big white weddings also deter cohabiting couples from marrying. Over one quarter of our long-term cohabiting mothers cited the expense of getting married as a reason for not marrying:

Neither of us are religious so we feel it would be hypocritical to be married in church. We also feel it's a great deal of expense which is wasted money when you think of the wedding dress and the reception and all that. You couldn't get married for under £4,000 and it's so much wasted money. 234/5531

We were going to get married last year but couldn't because I got pregnant again, so we had to postpone it until we could afford it again. The local vicar was very good and understanding. We just couldn't afford the expense and things with another baby on the way. 020/5973

Money for the wedding itself. 149/7275

The words of these long-term cohabiting mothers underline the continuing symbolic importance of the big, white wedding which, according to Gillis, has never been so popular, particularly among working-class couples who spend as much if not more on getting married as the wealthy.[15]

A big wedding has always been more than just a terrific party for family and friends. It is – or was – the major rite of passage for young women, when they pass through the door marked 'adult' and join their mothers on the other side.[16] It seemingly no longer matters that today brides are rarely virgins; nor indeed, that many are now mothers when they walk down the isle. It is the bride's big day. For many young women, it may be the *only* day when she is well and truly the centre of attention.

Elements of our characterisation of the importance of the big wedding may be traced in the actions of cohabiting mothers who turn away from *marriage* because of the expense of a *wedding*. Tradition tells them what a proper wedding is: *popular custom dictated an elaborate event, involving the huge expenditure of time and money.*[17] Lacking money, such young women choose cohabitation over a registry wedding, sensing the inadequacy of the latter: *Without all the festivities, no smallholder could consider himself or herself properly married.*[18] The question that remains for future research is whether these young cohabiting mothers, often with 2 or 3 children, are accepted as 'adults' by others, in the absence of the title 'wife'.

As it was the cost of a wedding which deterred these young cohabiting mothers from marrying, their comparatively poorer economic circumstances might have been expected. Among all long-term cohabiting mothers, those who cited the expense of marrying were the youngest (average age 28.6 years) and the most likely to be without qualifications (43 per cent). They were the least likely to be in paid work (29 per cent) or to own or be buying their own homes (38 per cent). One in 3 had an unemployed partner; over 40 per cent had household incomes of £12,000 or less. It was the case also that a small group of these mothers had higher-level qualifications (10 per cent) and household incomes above £24,000 (14 per cent), but these few apart, most long-term cohabiting mothers who had not married because of wedding costs were young, unqualified and unemployed women from working-class backgrounds.

Marriage delayed

In greatly different economic circumstances were the 1 in 5 women who were continuing to cohabit because they had not *yet* married:

> When we first moved in John wasn't divorced and we were happy the way we were. But now we have decided to get married in two months' time. 286/1680

> We never seem to get the time. We keep saying we ought. We sometimes say we'll do it and go to town and say we are, but by the time we've done the shopping we've never got round to it. 197/1795

> We always meant to. 183/1271

There was little sense of antipathy towards marriage in the words of those women who remained unmarried because one partner was not yet divorced or because they had not yet got around to marrying or for some other, similar reason. Nor was there much indication that a lack of money was a deterrent. Rather, the dominant impression was that these women were likely to marry sooner or later.

The women who expressed such views had lived with their partners for the shortest period of time (6.3 years) among our long-term cohabiting mothers and 1 in 4 had been married before. As likely to come from working-class homes (44 per cent) as cohabiting mothers who could not afford a wedding (43 per cent), their current economic circumstances differed markedly. None lived in households with no earners and 44 per cent lived in households where both partners were in paid work. Consequently, women expressing these views included the highest proportion of owner occupiers (75 per cent); while about 1 in 7 had a joint income in excess of £24,000 per year.

Fear of divorce

The final major reason we examine for not marrying differed in kind from the preceding three explanations in that it was not antipathy or indifference towards marriage that perpetuated their cohabitation, but an strong dislike of divorce. One in 3 women who reported this view had been married before; but it was not only her own divorce that might inform her views, but that also of her partner, parents or friends:

> Everyone in my family that have been married are divorced. I don't think it's worth getting married. To me it's a lot of pain getting married and breaking up. 046/1917

> I'm fairly anti-marriage – an awful lot of marriages end in divorce. I've not a lot of faith in the institution of marriage. My sister is divorced and a lot of friends are. It's not a lack of commitment to my partner, but I don't feel we need to be married. I take the idea of marriage very seriously. 196/2532

> Having been married before, the length of time it took me to get divorced really. Also, I'm not a religious person, so I don't see the point. He doesn't want to get married at all. 281/1951

Sometimes, fears raised by an earlier experience of divorce co-existed with worries about the stability of a current relationship:

> I was married before and it didn't work out. My first husband used to beat me up so I left him and he was also an alcoholic. We decided not just now – it's not suitable. We tend to fall out every so often and he goes back and stays with his mum so it's better the way it is. 084/0133

The economic circumstances of these long-term cohabiting mothers most closely resembled those of long-term cohabiting mothers who could not afford to marry. They tended to be older than other long-term cohabiting mothers (average age 32.3 years); and included the highest proportion of cohabiting mothers (55 per cent) with household incomes of £12,000 or less, and the lowest proportion (5 per cent) with household incomes over £24,000 per year. One in 3 households had no one in paid employment; 2 in 3 of the women themselves were out of the labour force. Over half of their partners worked now – or last worked – in manual jobs. Their circumstances and attitudes bring to mind vividly Parker's (1990) conjectural but seemingly accurate portrayal of modern-day cohabiting women:

> One can speculate that cohabitation might be attractive to [...] working class men and women in, say, their late 20s or early 30s [who] may find that their marriages have broken down and [that] they are reluctant to make the sort of commitments traditionally required of marriage. [...] Working class women who have been through a divorce might be prepared to form a new relationship but be slow to marry.

[...] income support may cease on cohabitation but at least the house is theirs.[19]

The advantages of cohabiting

One of our research concerns was to identify the advantages and disadvantages of cohabitation perceived by women who had experienced a period of living with a partner outside marriage. To ensure a wide range of such experience, we questioned all women who had cohabited with the fathers of their four year old child for some period, whether or not they had married subsequently, or when that marriage might have taken place, about the advantages and disadvantages of cohabitation when compared with marriage.[20] This meant that women whose experience of cohabitation had ended in marriage some 4 or more years before our interviews were asked the same questions as women who were continuing to cohabit with their partners; their responses, moreover, suggested that women's perceptions are affected the duration and outcome of their period of cohabitation.

Table 4.4 summarises the advantages outlined by women who had cohabited with their partners for some period, and indicates the average

Table 4.4   Advantages of cohabitation

Column percentages

	Long-term cohabiting mothers	Cohabited pre-maritally	
		Married after baby	Married before baby
No legal ties/more freedom	23	29	19
Able to test relationship/ trial marriage	3	20	30
Do not take relationship for granted	6	2	4
Double MIRAS	5	2	4
Able to retain individuality	3	4	4
Cheaper than marriage	1	0	4
None	60	55	54
Average duration of cohabitation (years)	7.8	4.2	1.9
Base:	*77*	*51*	*57*

Note: More than one answer possible.

duration of cohabitation experienced by each group. Advantages associated with cohabitation were reported by similar proportions of the three groups of women. Surprisingly, though, women who were *continuing* to cohabit were slightly less likely to say that there were advantages to cohabitation (40 per cent) than women who had subsequently married their partners (45 per cent).

Trial marriage

The figures presented in Table 4.4 suggest a link between the duration of cohabitation and the advantages that women perceive might inhere in such a relationship when compared with marriage. For women whose *pre-marital* cohabitation ended before the birth of any children, the primary advantage of cohabiting was to test their relationship with their partner before committing themselves to marriage. These women had lived with their husbands before marriage for a relatively short period – less than 2 years on average – and the benefit that many now recall about that period was that it was a trial marriage: a chance to

> get to know each other better. To get a better understanding of principles and attitudes to life, attitudes to children – fairly mundane things. 146/1843

It matters little whether or not these women *entered* into a cohabiting relationship in order to test its durability or for some other reason; what is apparent from their responses is that an inclination to treat living together as a trial marriage is likely to be associated with shortened durations of cohabitation. As cohabitation lengthens, moreover, the perception that it acts as a practice run for marriage tends to disappear. For example, women who were *continuing* to cohabit when interviewed were highly unlikely to suggest that an advantage of living together was that it allowed opportunities to test relationships. At least some of these women initially began to live with their partners with the expectation that they would marry; and it seems likely that many eventually will marry (see below). Regardless, their views after many years' cohabitation suggest that the advantages of this living arrangement lie elsewhere than as a test for marriage.

A sense of freedom

Of rather more importance for mothers who were *continuing* to cohabit, but only cited by just over 1 in 5, was the sense of freedom associated with cohabitation. It is worth noting that in this regard, cohabiting mothers did not differ substantially in their views from women who had cohabited and married *before* having children, among whom also about 1 in 5 cited the lack of legal ties as an advantage of cohabitation:

> You're not perhaps feeling as committed; or at least that you can alter the arrangements and get out of it if you need to. It's more easily broken. 280/5215 (married before baby born)

> You have not got to go through the courts if you are living together and anything goes wrong. You can just go your separate ways. My mum had two bad marriages and that's enough to put anybody off! 108/5438 (long-term cohabiting mother)

> I've not got to go through the courts etc. to get divorced. There's nothing stopping me, if I want to leave I can just leave. 046/1917 (long-term cohabiting mother)

The inherent incompatibility between the notion of a trial marriage and a wish for freedom from legal ties is sufficient to render coherent the responses of women who had cohabited but chose to marry before becoming mothers. However, it seems surprising that so few cohabiting mothers cited the lack of legal ties as an advantage of cohabitation, despite it being the most commonly cited advantage. We examine later the extent to which legal ties had been established between the children and partners of long-term cohabiting mothers. Here it may suffice to suggest that some ties develop independently of the legal relationship between couples, and a wish for freedom and independence might not sit well with being a parent, an outcome that was recognised by at least two long-term cohabiting mothers:

> Personally I just feel more independent not being married. It would be easier to go if things went wrong. No, actually, it probably wouldn't be any easier now that we have a child – it would be just as traumatic as being married and breaking up. 021/2032

> [There's a] greater *sense* of freedom – not a reality – you are no more free than if you were married. But you both know that there is no tie, so in a sense you are free. 044/4365

The disadvantages of cohabiting

Table 4.5 summarises the disadvantages of cohabiting in comparison with marrying as reported by women who had had some experience of living as part of a couple outside marriage. Women whose period of cohabitation was the most distant in time – those who cohabited but married *before* becoming mothers – were the least likely to report disadvantages associated with cohabitation (37 per cent); and women who had given up cohabiting for marriage more recently were the most likely to report disadvantages (45 per cent). These differences may reflect little more than the passage of time, as some women look backwards fondly towards that period of their lives when they had no children, no formal ties to their partners and few

Table 4.5   Disadvantages of cohabitation

Column percentages

| | Long-term cohabiting mothers | Cohabited pre-maritally | |
		Married after baby	Married before baby
No commitment/feel insecure	8	16	19
Socially unacceptable behaviour/ stigma against unmarried mothers	14	10	5
Children affected/father has no rights	10	10	14
Better tax/benefits if married	5	2	2
Official forms awkward	5	0	0
None	57	55	63
Base:	*77*	*51*	*57*

responsibilities, while others carry more recent memories of the problems that can attend unmarried family life. In any event, the differences were not large between these two groups of now-married women, and neither group differed markedly in their estimation of the disadvantages of cohabitation from mothers who continued to live outside marriage, among whom 43 per cent reported disadvantages.

Feelings of insecurity
The nature of the disadvantages cited by women with differing cohabitation and marital histories did not vary markedly, but here too links between the experience of cohabitation and perceived disadvantages were apparent. For example, cohabiting women who ultimately married were at least twice as likely as women who continued to cohabit to report feelings of insecurity or vulnerability – either their own or on behalf of their children – as a disadvantage of cohabitation. Nineteen per cent of women who married before becoming mothers and 16 per cent of those who married afterwards cited insecurity or lack of commitment as a disadvantage, compared with only 8 per cent of currently cohabiting mothers.

> One can feel a little insecure if not married. It's perhaps the way one's brought up. You feel better when everything is legal and official. 049/0586 (married after baby was born)

> Only where children are involved, I think. I think if you are not
> married and there are children, I think it is less secure for the children.
> 154/1000 (married before baby was born)

> If you have children, it's just better for the child, to be married
> beforehand. It's easier to split up with children involved than to get
> divorced. My parents were not married and I didn't feel secure.
> 048/0699 (married before baby was born)

It is, of course, only reasonable that cohabiting women who feel
vulnerable (personally or on behalf of their children) would be more likely
than women who do not share these feelings to put an end to uncertainty
by marrying. In this regard our findings are inherently plausible. But it is
worth noting also that only a minority of women – whatever their
cohabitation and marital histories – cited vulnerability or insecurity as a
disadvantage; when they did so, moreover, they were more likely to be
thinking of their children than themselves. It is perhaps a reflection of their
increased presence in the public domain, through paid employment, that so
few women felt insecure in their private lives simply by being unmarried.

Social unacceptability

Similar comments may be appropriate in relation to cohabitation as socially
unacceptable or stigmatised behaviour, particularly for women with
children. Table 4.5 indicates that this disadvantage was reported by only 5
per cent of women whose pre-marital cohabitation ended *before* they
became mothers; that is, by the group of cohabiting women *least* likely to
elicit the offending comments of others. Indeed, one such woman who had
crossed both ethnic and religious lines when she chose to cohabit, married
before having children in order to gain familial approval:

> Getting married wasn't a question then – it was the idea to get to know
> my partner and be sure I could live with him. Marriage just seemed a
> formality, a piece of paper. [...] Acceptance by members of our
> families – particularly mine as he's not from the same ethnic group
> or religion as I. I am Asian and he is Catholic. I think it's best to be
> married if you're going to start a family. 059/5272

In contrast, women whose behaviour had left them more open to the
criticisms of others – those who had cohabited *after* becoming mothers,
whether or not they ultimately married – were considerably more likely to
refer to the social unacceptability of cohabitation after motherhood:

> People do accept you and view you a lot better if you are married and
> have a child. We were looked down on as we weren't married and
> had a child. Thirty to thirty-five year olds were surprisingly the worst.
> Childminders refused us as we weren't married. 054/3244 (married
> after baby was born)

> Coming from a large international city to a small rural area, I found
> [I was] being constantly confronted with the expectation that you were
> married and then having to explain why you weren't. 233/3242
> (married after baby was born)

> Other people's attitudes – especially now we have children. Some of
> my family don't think it is permanent and there may be a stigma
> attached to the children's illegitimacy. 206/1494 (continuing to
> cohabit)

It remained only a minority, however, who cited social or family
disapproval as a disadvantage of cohabitation, encompassing 1 in 10 of
cohabiting women who married *after* having children and 1 in 7 of
long-term cohabiting mothers who had not (yet) married. Disapproval may
rankle a few, but it seemingly does not deter the many.

Other disadvantages

The other main disadvantage recorded in Table 4.5, that children may be
affected by cohabitation and that fathers may have no rights, was cited about
equally by the three groups of cohabiting women. Sometimes, this concern
was expressed in relation to differing surnames, particularly by women who
cohabited *after* motherhood:

> I was the only one with a different surname. We were worried about
> what the children would think when they grew up and realised they
> had different surnames. 030/6002 (married after baby was born)

> Not having the same name as my children. I feel like an outsider
> sometimes. 159/5458 (continuing to cohabit)

> Not having the same name. When the children got to school and when
> we go to school for reports and such like, and the children have my
> name – my partner must feel hurt. 234/5531 (continuing to cohabit)

Other mothers worried about the financial disadvantages of
cohabitation breakdown and how this might affect their children:

> If it breaks down, the woman might not be working or earning as much
> as she would have been, and so the children might suffer. 154/1000
> (married before baby was born)

The fact that fathers in cohabiting relationships might lack parental
rights was mentioned by a small number of women in each group, and was
seen as a potential disadvantage of cohabitation. We discuss this issue more
fully in Chapter 6 and save until then the particular comments made by
women who expressed a concern about legal relationships. But before
leaving the discussion of disadvantages, it is fair to note that at least some
of the drawbacks to cohabitation mentioned by women who were

continuing to cohabit appeared to rank higher as inconveniences than as serious impediments to living as a couple outside marriage:

> It makes filling in forms complicated because sometimes they count you as a couple and sometimes they don't. None other [disadvantages] that I've come across or anticipate. 225/5077

> Just having to explain why and filling in forms. Just inconvenience, really. 230/6727

> Introducing yourself to people, explaining what the relationship is. 277/5566

It appears vexing that so far neither our language nor our bureaucracies have caught up entirely with changes in the way people organise their lives.

Notes
1. Jessie Bernard, *The Future of Marriage*, Bantam Books 1972 (4th edition 1978), pp.87-8.
2. Christine Delphy and Diane Leonard, *Familiar Exploitation: A New Analysis of Marriage in Contemporary Western Societies*, Polity Press, 1992, p.265.
3. Haskey, op.cit., 1992, pp 14-17.
4. Michael Anderson, Frank Bechhofer and Steve Kendrick, 'Individual and Household Strategies: Some Empirical Evidence from The SCELI', manuscript, no date, pp.21-22.
5. J. Burgoyne, *Cohabitation and Contemporary Family Life*, ESRC End of Grant Report, unpublished, 1985.
6. Anderson et al, op.cit., p.22.
7. Women who married straight away, without a period of pre-marital cohabitation were not asked this question.
8. The responses shown in the table come from a question in the self-completion questionnaire which offered respondents pre-selected answers. Respondents were invited to tick as many of these answers as they wished and to write in any further answers. The question itself replicates one used in SCELI.
9. Among both long-term cohabiting mothers, and cohabiting women who married *after* having children, the previously-married were more likely to suggest that they set up home together because they were in love. For long-term cohabiting mothers, this response was the only one given by more than 4 of the 18 formerly-married women. Eleven formerly married women gave this response.
10. Marrying for love, freely chosen, is said to be a hallmark of modern Western society, particularly when contrasted with (probably mythical) past times when marriages were social and economic unions (cf. Penny Mansfield and Jean Collard, *The Beginning of the Rest of your Life?*, Macmillan, 1988). We would argue that most women marry or establish relationships because they love a particular man, rather than some other man. As an explanation for becoming a couple, love is appropriate and socially acceptable, to oneself and to others. However, we would also agree with Delphy and Leonard, who reason that behind love lie the social and economic advantages of conforming to the norm and of allying oneself with a

member of the dominant group: sharing his income and getting protection. (op.cit., 1992, p.265)

11. 'The effect of housing costs on young people's lifestyles', Joseph Rowntree Foundation *Housing Research Findings* No 68, October 1992.

12. Respondents were asked the following open-ended question: "We'd also like to know why you chose to live together as a couple, rather than get married straight away. What things would you say were important in influencing your decision to delay getting married?"

    Up to 20 different responses were coded, and ultimately collapsed into the categories shown in Table 4.2. Responses were analysed so that close meanings given by the same respondent were not doubled counted. The table sums to more than 100 per cent because respondents were able to give more than one answer.

13. Haskey, op.cit., p.12.

14. Cohabiting respondents were asked the following open-ended question: "We are also interested in why you and your partner have chosen not to get married. What things would you say were important in influencing your decision not to get married?"

    Fourteen different responses were coded and ultimately collapsed into the categories shown in Table 4.3. Of the 77 cohabiting respondents, 44 gave one reason, 26 gave 2 reasons, 5 gave 3 reasons and 2 gave 4 reasons. Responses were analysed so that close meanings given by the same respondent were not doubled counted. The table sums to more than 100 per cent because respondents were able to give more than one answer.

15. Gillis, op.cit., p.311.

16. cf. Davidoff and Hall, op.cit., 1987; Gittens, op.cit., 1993.

17. Gillis, op.cit., p.84.

18. Ibid. p.84.

19. Parker, op.cit., p.124.

20. Women were asked "Do you think there are any advantages (disadvantages) in living together as a couple, compared with being married?" Women who responded positively were then asked "What do you think the advantages (disadvantages) are? Women who had separated from their partner by the time of our interviews were not asked these questions.

5   Cohabitation or marriage? – marriage

Our focus now turns towards marriage and the women who were still cohabiting when interviewed. About 40 per cent of our long-term cohabiting mothers expected to marry their partners someday, one-quarter thought that they might marry, and just less than one-third had no intention of marrying. We examine below the factors that might precipitate marriage for these women and the extent to which they have experienced pressure to marry. But to put their views into context, we turn first to the experiences of the *married* women included in the study.

Married women and marriage

It is worth reminding ourselves that the three groups of married women we interviewed experienced cohabitation, marriage and motherhood differently. Two of these groups are familiar already: women who cohabited and ultimately married, the first lot *before* motherhood and the second lot *after* motherhood. The average length of time spent cohabiting by women who married before having children was 23 months; and just over 4 years by women who married after having children. The views of the third group of women have yet to be incorporated into our discussions, which have focused largely on cohabitation rather than on marriage. This group encompasses women who did not live with their husbands before marriage; accordingly, none became mothers before marrying. The average length of time they had been married at the time of our interviews was 11 years.

We note in Chapter 2 that the relative sizes of the group of women who were *continuing* to cohabit and the group who had married *after* having children was determined largely by the timing of our research. That is, if we had interviewed one year later or six months earlier, the numbers included in these two groups would be different, as more or fewer cohabiting mothers would have moved from cohabiting-motherhood into married-motherhood. We raise this point here because of its relevance to the discussion of the decision to marry. Our findings suggest that there is a steady flow of cohabiting couples into marriage. The (essentially

Table 5.1 The flow into marriage of women who married after becoming mothers

			Cumulative column percentages
Per cent married by:	%	(N)	Duration of cohabitation after birth of 4 year old
End December 1988	27	(14)	1 year
June 1989	43	(22)	18 months
End December 1989	59	(30)	2 years
End December 1990	76	(39)	3 years
End December 1991	90	(46)	4 years
June 1992	100	(51)	4½ years

unanswerable) question which this finding gives rise to is whether all cohabiting couples will ultimately marry (or separate), or whether there exists a core who would choose always to remain outside formal marriage.

The timing of marriage among women who married *after* having at least one child brought to our attention the steady flow from cohabiting-motherhood into married-motherhood. Table 5.1 summarises the proportions marrying at various intervals after the birth of the 4 year old child who precipitated participation in our initial research. The table focuses on the passage of time since the 4 year old's birth (rather than the birth of any earlier children) because it was on the basis of their marital status *at that point* that both women who had continued to cohabit and those who had married after becoming mothers were designated 'cohabiting mothers'. Only after our interviews in June 1992 was this one group of women separated into two groups. The rather smooth flow of 'cohabiting mothers' into marriage captured by Table 5.1 highlights the transient nature of cohabitation for most women, and places into perspective the highly unusual long-term and continuing cohabitation explored in this study.

The decision to marry

Table 5.2 brings together the various factors which influenced the decisions of women to marry.[1] At one level, the table can be regarded as a summary of differences in women's attitudes which tends to reflect their circumstances prior to marriage. For example, the most important reason for marrying given by cohabiting women who married *after* becoming mothers was to ensure the security of their children. Over two-thirds of cohabiting women who married *after* having children gave this response compared with 28 per cent of their counterparts who married *before*

Table 5.2   Factors influencing decision to marry

Column percentages

| | Cohabited pre-maritally | | Non-cohabiting married mothers |
	Married after baby	Married before baby	
Own security	41	33	41
Children's security	69	28	14
Fell in love	12	39	65
Parents wanted us to marry	10	18	17
Religious reasons	2	7	15
To make a commitment	57	53	62
Could afford a house	0	10	17
Pregnancy	8	16	11
Wanted a child *	10	40	26
Children wanted us to marry	8	2	1
She/he became legally free to marry	18	19	1
Base:	*51*	*57*	*92*

*   Excluding women who indicated that pregnancy was precipitating factor in decision to marry.

becoming mothers and 14 per cent of women who did not cohabit prior to marrying. This does not mean that women who married before becoming mothers cared less about their children's security. Indeed, our findings suggest the opposite: among the disadvantages of cohabitation perceived by women who married before motherhood was an adverse impact on children's security and well-being; while one-quarter of the women who never cohabited cited children's security as an advantage of marriage. Rather, the explanation for the large difference in responses is likely to be quite simple: marrying *before* having children means that one does not need to get married *after* they are born in order to ensure their security and well-being. All three groups of married mothers were concerned to protect their children; what differed among them was the stage at which formal marriage became part of that protection.

Indeed, because of the differing histories of cohabitation, marriage and motherhood of the three groups of women included in Table 5.2, the findings it presents are as much about the *timing* of marriage as about potential influences upon marriage. That is, some influences appear to be common to marriage, whatever its timing relative to cohabitation and motherhood. A wish for the personal security that marriage brings or a desire to make a public commitment, for example, was cited by roughly similar proportions of women, as was the influence of parents' wishes. In other words, similar influences affect women's decisions to marry – a sense of commitment to their partners, their own or their children's security, parents' wishes – but the *timing* of marriage in relation to becoming a couple and becoming a parent may be determined by other, more diverse factors.

This point may be partly illustrated by reference to 'falling in love'. Table 5.2 shows that almost two-thirds of women who did not cohabit with their husbands before marriage cited love as an important influence on their decision to marry. But reference back to Table 4.1, which summarises influences on the decision to cohabit, suggests that falling in love was a roughly similar influence on the decisions of women who pre-maritally cohabited to start living with their partners. That is, the impetus to become a couple stemmed from a similar source, what differed was the initial place given to formal marriage in that relationship.

Table 5.2 gives a partial view of the factors which might distinguish between those who marry at the beginning of a relationship and those for whom marriage is delayed until after a period of cohabitation or until after motherhood. A prior marriage is an obvious delaying factor. Women who cohabited before marriage were substantially more likely than non-cohabiting women to report that the timing of their marriage was influenced by the fact that they or their partner had become legally free to marry again. Almost 1 in 5 women who had pre-maritally cohabited gave this response compared with only 1 per cent of women who did not live with their husbands before marriage. The continuing existence of an earlier marriage might explain (at least partially) why one couple who fell in love might marry immediately while another only begins to cohabit.

Religious beliefs are a second obvious influence on the decision to marry and the timing of marriage. Common knowledge and demographic evidence suggest that couples with strong religious beliefs are more likely to marry than to cohabit[2] – a pattern that is borne out by the findings in Table 5.2. Non-cohabiting women were the most likely (15 per cent) to cite religion as an important influence on their decision to marry, and cohabiting women who married *after* motherhood the least likely to do so (2 per cent). Indeed, among the latter, religion appeared to be a negligible influence at best, and only 6 per cent reported that they attended an act of worship at least once a week compared with 17 per cent of non-cohabiting women.

Pregnancy is a third obvious influence on marriage, albeit like religion, of diminishing importance for many women. Table 5.2 indicates that, unlike women who married *after* having children, pregnancy appeared to act as an incentive to marry among cohabiting women who married *before* having children and non-cohabiting women, of whom 16 per cent and 11 per cent, respectively, reported that pregnancy was an important influence on their decision to marry.

The reasons why cohabiting women who married *after* having children did not marry earlier were discussed in Chapter 4. What is of interest here is that although a first (and often unplanned) pregnancy was not seen by these women as sufficient reason to marry, a second or third pregnancy may have been – particularly if it was attended by pressure from family. Eight per cent of women who married *after* having children reported that a pregnancy had them influenced to marry (Table 5.2). For these women, however, marriage came between births rather than before motherhood:

> Then when I was pregnant, with my second child, we had a lot of hassle from parents to get married. 188/4794

> [pressure to get married came from] my mother, when I was expecting my third child. 173/5665

Long-term cohabiting women and marriage

We saw in Table 5.1 that there was a steady flow from cohabiting-motherhood into married-motherhood among women who married sometime *after* having children, and we surmised that had our research been carried out at an earlier or later point, the relative size of our group of long-term cohabiting mothers would have changed – its dimension being determined by the timing of our research rather than by influences directly relevant to cohabiting mothers themselves. Thus, we would expect *a priori* that a substantial proportion of our cohabiting mothers would intend to marry someday; and, indeed, this proved to be the case. Of the 77 long-term cohabiting mothers included in our study, about 40 per cent reported that they expected to marry their partners someday, one-quarter thought that they might marry someday, and just less that one-third had no intention of marrying (5 women did not answer the question).

Table 5.3 summarises selected characteristics of long-term cohabiting mothers according to their expectations of marriage, and reveals a number of findings of interest. First, the longer women have cohabited, the less likely they are to marry. Women who reported that they positively expected to marry someday had lived with their partners just over 7 years on average, a duration which stretched to 8.5 years among cohabiting mothers who reported that they had no intention of marrying.

Secondly, employed women were less likely to express an intention to marry than women not in paid work. Fewer than half (48 per cent) of those

Table 5.3   **Selected characteristics of long-term cohabiting women according to their marriage expectations**

Column percentages

		Expects to marry some day	
	Yes	Perhaps	No
Average years cohabiting	7.06	8.07	8.5
Average number of children	2.2	2.4	1.8
Women's average age	29.5	31.9	31.5
% Women married before	30	16	17
% With partner married before	27	32	35
% Women without qualifications	37	32	26
% Women not in paid work	60	63	48
Base:	*30*	*19*	*23*

who reported that they did not intend to marry were out of the labour force, compared with 60 per cent or more of those who expected to marry or thought that they might marry someday. This may reflect the comparatively better chances for financial independence of women who remain in the labour market during family formation; alternatively, being employed might engender a stronger sense of personal independence and the desire not to jeopardize this through marriage.

The third finding of interest to emerge from Table 5.3 concerns the impact of a previous marriage on women's current marriage expectations. Somewhat surprisingly, the earlier marriage of her partner appeared to have more effect on a cohabiting woman's marriage intentions than her own previous marriage. Over one-third of women who reported that they did not intend to marry had partners who had been married before, compared with only 17 per cent who had themselves been married previously. Perhaps there are more optimists among long-term cohabiting women than among long-term cohabiting men? Or might it be the cohabiting *mother* reporting here, acknowledging the potential importance of marriage for the security of her children? It is certainly the case, as we indicate below, that providing security for children was paramount among the factors that might influence cohabiting mothers to marry. A concern for her children might, then, account for the apparently greater willingness of long-term cohabiting mothers to allow the *triumph of hope over experience*.

Table 5.4   Factors which might influence a long-term cohabiting mother's decision to marry

Column percentages

	All	Expects to marry some day	
		Yes	Uncertain/perhaps
Own security	35	43	21
Children's security	71	80	58
Parents' wishes	14	20	5
Children's wishes	51	50	53
To make a further commitment	47	50	42
Base:	*49*	*30*	*19*

Note: More than one answer was permitted.

Reasons to marry

Table 5.4 summarises the considerations which might influence the decision of long-term cohabiting mothers to marry, and distinguishes between the answers given by those who said they expected to marry some day and those who were uncertain.[3] Of considerable interest is the pre-eminence given to the security of children as a likely influence on the decision of cohabiting mothers to marry. Overall, 71 per cent of cohabiting mothers cited their children's security as a reason to marry, rising to 80 per cent of women who positively expected to marry their partners.[4] In the strength of their responses, long-term cohabiting mothers excelled even women who married *after* having children, among whom 69 per cent cited their children's security as an important influence upon their decision to marry (see Table 5.2). The closeness of their responses gives added substance to our portrayal of a continuous flow from cohabiting-motherhood into married-motherhood. It seems evident that had we returned to our cohabiting mothers in the months following our interviews, we would have found a yet-smaller pool who were continuing to remain outside formal marriage.

Mothers who were continuing to cohabit additionally resembled women who had married *after* having children in placing their children's security ahead of their own security as a reason for marrying. In all, personal security was cited by 35 per cent of long-term cohabiting mothers, rising to 43 per cent of those who positively expected to marry their partners someday. Other potential influences on the decisions of cohabiting mothers to marry included their parents, their children and the desire to make a further commitment to their partner. Only two long-term cohabiting mothers put forward reasons to marry not encompassed by the factors included in Table 5.4.

Pressure to marry

When we were designing our research into the lives and experiences of cohabiting mothers it seemed reasonable to expect that a fair degree of pressure to marry would be reported by women who chose to maintain a family life outside the bonds of formal marriage. Society has changed, we agreed, but surely not so much that women – and particularly, mothers – can break normative rules with impunity. In carrying out our research, however, we had to modify our views somewhat. When and if the long-term cohabiting mothers we interviewed marry, it seems likely that the large majority will do so in the *absence* of overt, external pressures. When asked if they had ever felt under any pressure to get married, only 10 long-term cohabiting mothers replied that they had, with 84 per cent replying negatively. Such pressure as was applied largely came from family and friends:

> Parents and friends – 'When are you two getting married?' 'It's about time you two got married.' 135/5779

> My mother – she said I should change name by deed poll if I was not getting married. My partner's mother - little comments. My sister – she wants to arrange it! 149/7275

Only rarely, however, did the force of such pressure lead to serious conflicts between family members:

> My parents, well just my father, not my mother. At first he stopped having any contact with me after the birth of my daughter – that lasted for about three years. He has now given up and we've resumed contact. I always made first moves and I kept in touch regularly and he eventually realised after death of his own mother that life is too short, so now we have a good relationship. 021/2032

Perhaps unexpectedly, women who married *after* having children were no more likely to report having felt under any pressure to marry than mothers who continued to cohabit (with 80 per cent of the former and 84 per cent of the latter responding negatively to our query). Women who married *after* having children were, however, more likely to mention 'people in general' or 'society' as the source of the pressure that they had experienced.

Of course, it is possible that since being married, some women will have forgotten the outside pressures that may have influenced their decisions to marry. But given the consistency of responses between these two groups of 'cohabiting mothers' this seems doubtful, and a more likely explanation would be that external pressure has come to play only a minor role in the decision of cohabiting mothers to marry. If this is indeed the case, then our study provides clear evidence of normative change.

However, pressure to marry may also come from *within* a cohabiting mother, particularly if she is concerned about the effects that cohabitation might have on her children. Accordingly, we asked women who had cohabited after becoming mothers if they thought that not being legally married affected, or would have affected, their children in any way. Among those who were *continuing* to cohabit, the consensus overwhelmingly was that children largely were unaffected by having cohabiting parents. Eighty-four per cent of still-cohabiting mothers replied in this way, with only 8 per cent positive that children could be affected and 8 per cent uncertain about the impact on children.

The concerns felt by mothers often focused on the treatment their children might receive at school, particularly from other children. Sometimes concern for their children was diffuse, other times it appeared strong enough to lead to marriage:

> It isn't the norm. They all want to be like the others at school. Other parents are married and they want their parents married. 286/1680

> School children can be quite cruel although I don't think these days it's very unusual. I can't think of any other ways it will affect her. 235/2235

> I don't really know – it's just a funny feeling at the back of my head somewhere. I just don't know. 014/3999

> By wondering why – doubting that we haven't loved each other enough to do that [get married]. They might not understand how much we love each other. I'd never want them to feel threatened by our not being married and feel daddy might go. Other children might say something to them and upset them. I wouldn't like my children to drop into a relationship and think it's the normal thing to do to live with someone. It's a moral issue I feel, I suppose. [My partner] wants us to get married now. 193/3343

But however strong the concerns of these mothers were, we do well to remember that they were expressed by only a small number of those who were *continuing* to cohabit. In contrast, almost one-third of cohabiting women who married *after* having children thought that their children might have been affected by their cohabitation. This may, of course, be part of the reasons why these women had chosen to marry. Interestingly, the actual concerns expressed by cohabiting mothers who had married did not differ in substance from those expressed by still-cohabiting mothers; only their consequences differed:

> It's what they might have to go through from other children when they start school. Names they might be called. 318/0744 (married after baby born)

> The fact that I had a different surname, as they got older, would have seemed strange. They would have realised they were not legitimate. 049/0586 (married after baby born)

> I don't know how it would but I didn't want him to feel the odd one out. I'd have to explain why his name was different to mine. 233/3242 (married after baby born)

> Insecurity. They were thrilled when we got married. 291/2526 (married after baby born)

The number of cohabiting mothers (married or otherwise) who reported feeling pressure to marry or adverse consequences for children in the absence of legal marriage was too small to be more than suggestive. Bearing this in mind, we might speculate that a disinclination to see pressure to marry stemming from society, the community or people in general, encourages the view that children will not be harmed by the decision not to marry. If pressure to marry comes mainly or only from family and friends – as reported by still-cohabiting mothers – then it is probable that children largely would be unaffected as grandparents, aunts, uncles and so on would be unlikely to take their displeasure out on the children, whatever their view of the parents' marital arrangements.

If, however, pressure to marry was felt to stem mainly from 'society' or 'people in general' – as reported by cohabiting women who married *after* becoming mothers – then concern about the implications of cohabiting for one's children seems an obvious outcome, and marriage an obvious solution.

Notes

1. The responses shown in the table come from a question in the self-completion questionnaire which offered respondents pre-selected answers. Respondents were invited to tick as many of these answers as they wished and to write in any further answers. The question itself replicates one used in SCELI.

2. John Haskey and David Coleman, for example, report that couples who marry in a civil ceremony are over three times more likely to have cohabited before marriage than couples who have a religious wedding. See 'Cohabitation before marriage: a comparison of information from marriage registration and the GHS', *Population Trends*, No. 43 (Spring) 1986, pp 15-17.

3. Women who said that they did not intend to marry were not asked about potential influences on the decision to marry.

4. Long-term cohabiting mothers who had been married before particularly were likely to name their children's security (11 women out of 18) and their children's wishes (8 out of 18) as influences upon their decisions to marry.

6 Family life

In this chapter, we address three questions which focus on the family lives of cohabiting mothers. First, we ask whether cohabiting couples and their children are 'families' in the legal sense: have they established a legal relationship between father and child? And if not, why not? Secondly, we ask whether they are 'families' socially: do mother, father and children all use the same family name in order to identify themselves as a family to the outside world? Are there any consequences of not using the same family name? Finally, we examine whether cohabiting families differ in any important respects from married families: are they more egalitarian, for example; or more companionate, or happier? What, if any, are the consequences of being unmarried for family life?

Families in law?

When a child is born to a married couple, the mother and father have equal and independent parental rights and authority. In the case of a child born to unmarried parents, the mother has exclusive rights. In other words, the fathers of children born to unmarried couples have no automatic parental rights, and joint registration of the birth does not confer such rights.[1] Under the provisions of the Family Law Reform Act 1987 – replaced by the Children Act 1989 – an unmarried father may apply to the court for an order giving him all parental rights and duties. The Children Act 1989 continues to offer cohabiting parents the option of seeking parental rights for fathers through the courts. But in addition, an unmarried couple may make a 'parental responsibility agreement' which, if made and recorded correctly, will confer parental responsibility on the father of the child.[2]

We addressed the issue of father's rights directly in our research.[3] Mothers who were continuing to cohabit and those who had married their partners sometime *after* the birth of their 4 year old child were asked a series of questions designed to uncover any legal arrangements that had been made between father and child; and in the absence of such arrangements, the reasons why no legal steps had been taken.

Table 6.1 **Extent to which cohabiting mothers established legal relationship between child and father**

	Still cohabiting	Married after having children
		Column percentages
Established formal legal relationship	0	0
Will naming partner as guardian	5	2
Written maintenance agreement in case of separation	3	0
Child named in father's passport	1	0
Base:	*77*	*41**

* Ten cohabiting women who married after they had had children were not asked this question.

The questions we put to cohabiting mothers were as follows: whether they had ever gone to the courts for an order giving their partners 'parental rights'; if they had ever drawn up a formal legal agreement giving their partners 'parental responsibility'; whether they had made any other written agreement with their partners; if they had done anything else. Women who replied negatively to the first three of these questions were then asked why they had not taken steps to create a legal relationship between their partners and children.

In the event, we were considerably surprised to discover that *none* of the women who were *continuing* to cohabit nor any of those who had married *after* having children had taken steps to establish either parental rights or parental responsibility for their partners. All but two woman reported that their child had been jointly registered by mother and father. A small number had written wills naming their partners as guardians of their children. But the overwhelming majority had taken no steps whatsoever to create the type of legal relationship between father and child which is conferred automatically by marriage. These findings are summarised in Table 6.1.

Table 6.2 brings together the reasons given by still-cohabiting mothers and cohabiting women who married *after* having children to explain their inaction. Priest suggests that applications by cohabiting fathers are likely to be uncommon because of the following necessary conditions. In order to seek parental rights or responsibility, cohabiting parents would need to: (a) realise that the father has no automatic parental rights, even though he *de facto* exercises such rights; (b) consider his lack of rights to be a problem; (c) know that a remedy exists to deal with the problem; (d) decide that it is

Table 6.2   Reasons why no legal relationship established between father and child

Column percentages

	Long-term cohabiting mothers	Cohabited pre-maritally Married AFTER baby born
Never thought about it	31	8
Considered it unnecessary	57	95
Father is 'real' father	6	10
Child has father's name	3	5
Birth registered by father	6	10
Thought it was automatic	13	10
Child/father have good relationship	10	18
Just not necessary	14	25
Plan to marry	1	13
Other reasons	12	0
Prefer informality	3	
Don't know how	3	
Would if separated	3	
Haven't got around to it yet	3	
Base:	*77*	*41**

Note: Sums to more than 100 because more than one answer possible

*   Ten cohabiting women who married after were not asked this question.

worth spending time, money and effort to seek a court order to bring their legal position into line with the reality of their daily lives. In Priest's view, if cohabiting parents do take steps to establish parental rights or responsibility for fathers, they will be likely to do so from a principled position of parental equality rather than because of any immediate practical problems.[4]

Each of the reasons outlined by Priest why cohabiting fathers might not seek parental rights or responsibility may be found in the responses of women who had cohabited as mothers. Well over half (57 per cent) of mothers who were *continuing* to cohabit and 95 per cent of cohabiting women who married *after* having children thought that it was not necessary to establish a legal relationship between father and child, often because they were ignorant of the law. About one-third of still-cohabiting mothers simply had never thought of doing so; again, often because they were unaware that such steps needed to be taken, or could be taken:

> Because she has her father's name and that makes it legal, so there's no need to do anything else. 042/6740 (continuing to cohabit)

> Well, he's her father – doesn't that give him parental responsibility? 037/2070 (continuing to cohabit)

> Because my daughter has my husband's surname. So from a legal point of view we don't need to do anything else. It is a legal document, the birth certificate. 040/0242 (continuing to cohabit)

> I didn't think it was necessary because we were together, I could see us as a family unit. It was the natural thing I thought, we're together aren't we? I didn't realise we had to do anything. We made the commitment to each other by having our daughter. 089/4773 (married after baby was born)

Of course, cohabiting women who married *after* having children had, by that marriage, established a legal relationship between father and child.[5] Indeed, for about 1 in 8 of these women, the fact that they intended marriage conditioned their belief that legal action was not needed:

> Because we were living together and we planned we would get married one day, so it wasn't necessary to do any of those things. 156/1165 (married after baby was born)

Our findings suggest that a substantial number of currently-cohabiting mothers do not understand the legal position of their partner vis-a-vis their children. In the views of the women we interviewed, establishing a legal relationship between father and child was unnecessary either because they believed that it happened automatically (13 per cent), because the child was acknowledged by the father (6 per cent) or had his name (3 per cent), or because the father had jointly registered the child's birth (6 per cent). In all of these cases, the women we interviewed were mistaken about the legal implications of remaining unmarried.

Moreover, a substantial proportion of the still-cohabiting mothers who reported that they had never thought about establishing a legal relationship between father and child, also exhibited ignorance of the law:

> I never thought about it. I didn't realise until we received a leaflet from my son's school that he hadn't got legal rights. 286/1680

> We haven't even thought about it. In fact, we are at present arranging for somebody else to be responsible for our children should anything happen to us. However, we had not realised that John was not legally responsible for our children as well as me. We will probably talk to the solicitor when we next see him. 221/1694

Cohabiting partners are likely to experience the consequences of fathers having neither parental rights nor parental responsibility only if their cohabiting relationship breaks down or their partner dies or is taken into custody.[6] In these circumstances, cohabiting fathers might find that they are denied access to, or custody of, their own children; and cohabiting mothers might find their intentions ignored. Sometimes, the children of cohabiting mothers will themselves suffer if they are denied their legitimate financial claims:[7]

> There were no reasons. At that time, we did not think it was necessary, that having his name on the birth certificate was adequate. Looking back now, after my partner's death, we would have been able to claim on my partner's estate. Probably having done something as simple as making a will, but with being a cohabitation and an illegitimate child, there was no claim I could make. [...] I would advise anyone in a cohabitation to make a will, at least to protect the child's financial interests – but you don't think of that when you're in your twenties. 249/0986

On these findings, there seems to be good reasons for arguing that there is a need for much better information, more widely available, about the rights – or, more accurately, the lack of rights of cohabiting fathers.

However, not all long-term cohabiting mothers were unaware of the need to take positive steps if they wished there to be a formal, legal relationship between their partner and children. For some (10 per cent) the stable and harmonious relationship that existed between father and child led them to believe that it was unnecessary to establish a legal relationship. Others (3 per cent) preferred the informality of cohabitation. And others still (3 per cent) simply had not got around to it yet. The views of some of these cohabiting mothers are expressed below:

> To me there is no need. He knows they are his children and he takes good care of them. 020/5972

> We see no need, it will not effect the child and we both know what we want from our relationship so we can discuss it. We don't need a legal relationship. 328/0946

> I don't think it's necessary. Don't see why he should have to just because we are not married. [...] we have had this thing through from school saying mother has the 'parental responsibility'. Because Dave and I are not married he has not got any parental responsibility. He is no less a father because we are not married. I do not think you should have to get married just to give husband parental rights, it should be the other way round. 029/2152

> I've never seen the need to have one. If we did split up I would naturally give him equal rights. 053/2488

And, as suggested also by Priest and confirmed below by at least one still-cohabiting mother, the effort involved in bringing the legal position of a cohabiting father into line with the reality of his daily life may mean that it never gets done:

> Time has not permitted. One day we will get round to sorting it out. But it is one of those jobs where we know we don't have a problem so we tend to put it to back of the pile of jobs to be done. 044/4365

It was the case, then, that none of the long-term cohabiting mothers we interviewed had taken the steps needed to create the type of legal relationship between father and child which occurs automatically with marriage. Consequently, one could make the argument that, strictly speaking, these women, their children and partners were not 'families' as this term is understood in law. But in addition to being on possibly dubious ground legally,[8] our findings so far suggest that arguing that view would bring forth considerable opposition from cohabiting mothers themselves. For a minority, cohabitation did appear to provide a preferred, looser relationship:

> I don't want to get married – I have more chance of keeping the children if we split up. 245/4916

> [Doesn't want legal relationship between father and child] because if I ever wanted to leave I could take the children easier. 246/4555

> I'd feel that he would own me if we were married. 139/1964

> I always feel if you're married you've got to do what your husband tells you, whereas if you're living together you can go out and do your own thing without asking permission. 084/0133

But for the majority of cohabiting mothers, their family lives were *family* lives, in fact, if not in law.

Families in name?

> You don't necessarily have to get married to be recognised as a family and spoken for. I am not married but I wear wedding rings. 068/6665

One of our interests was to examine the extent to which cohabiting mothers might 'disguise' their cohabitation by using the same family name as their partners. The young still-cohabiting mother quoted above, for example, not only wears wedding rings but she and her children all use her partner's surname: a family in law, perhaps not; a family in name, without doubt.

Table 6.3 summarises the distribution of family names used by women and children in each of our three groups of mothers with some experience

Table 6.3   Family names used by respondent, child and partner/husband

Column percentages

	Long-term cohabiting mothers	Cohabited pre-maritally	
		Married after baby	Married before baby
All use partner/husband's name	21	96	97
Mother uses her name/ partner uses his name; and			
Child uses both	7	0	0
Child uses mother's	9	0	0
Child uses father's	63	2	2
All use mother's name	0	1	0
All use combination of mother's and partner's	0	1	1
Base:	*77*	*51*	*57*

of cohabitation.[9] One finding of note that emerges is the overwhelming unanimity among *married* women about taking their husband's name as their own: over 95 per cent reported that mother, father and children all used the same family name, that of their husbands. Our suggestion that families define themselves socially by presenting a single unit with a single name is, on these findings, well supported.

However, the large majority of cohabiting couples and their children presented themselves to the outside world, not under the umbrella of a single family name, but as bearing a selection of names. Only about 1 in 5 women who were continuing to cohabit reported that mother, father and child all used the same name, that of her partner, although others indicated that they intended to adopt this course eventually:

> We are quite happy as we are – so many marriages end in divorce. I will change my name one day but do not intend to get married. 205/1963

> People tend to assume I'm Mrs Jones at nursery school when I take my son. I would like to have the same name as my kids have. I've been thinking of changing it by deed poll. The officials at nursery or health visitors, when they see me coming, they say loudly 'It's Johnny Jones's mum!' [...] I would like people to call me by my partner's name – it would be better for the kids. 178/6658

The far more common approach, reported by 63 per cent, was for long-term cohabiting mothers to retain their own names and for children and fathers to use his name. A further 7 per cent of cohabiting mothers reported that their children used a combination of mother's and father's names. Only in about 1 in 10 cohabiting families did children use just their mother's name.

In a society, moreover, where over 95 per cent of married women take their husband's name, having too many names can cause problems, as we saw first in Chapter 4 when reporting on the perceived disadvantages of cohabitation:

> Different surnames, I still feel a bit embarrassed. 149/0133 (continuing to cohabit)

> It's very confusing name-wise. We never know what to call each other just social-wise. 183/1271 (continuing to cohabit)

> My mother-in-law keeps saying we ought to get married. She says the children have got his name, why not me. 042/6740 (continuing to cohabit)

Still-cohabiting mothers were not alone in referring to difficulties associated with differing family names: women who married *after* having children had experienced similar problems. Indeed, for some of these women it seems likely that such problems influenced their decision to marry:

> It was complicated for the children to have a different name to mine. Children don't like to be different. 223/3377 (married after baby was born)

> The community, the local community, their expectations that we were married and their shock when they discovered we'd not got the same name and then feeling that I should explain that they were our children. 233/3242 (married after baby was born)

The attention given to family names by mothers who were *continuing* to cohabit and by those who had married *after* becoming mothers caught us, as researchers, somewhat by surprise: it seemed from these women's accounts that 30 years and more of the women's movement has had little or no impact on British ways of thinking about marriage and the family. Moreover, had we undertaken our research in Latin America, Spain or Portugal, this particular problem would not have arisen at all, as traditions there demand that married women retain their own family names. Here, however, other traditions hold sway; and do so with apparent imperviousness to the changes taking place in British families' lives.[10]

Families just the same?

We turn now to examine more directly the family lives of long-term cohabiting couples (as reported by cohabiting mothers) and ask whether these differed in any important ways from the lives of married couples. Are cohabiting couples more egalitarian than couples who marry, for example? Or more likely to share outside interests or problems? Given a chance to live their lives over, would cohabiting women choose the same partner? Are they more or less happy than married mothers? In other words, are families *families* just the same, whatever their legal arrangements, or do cohabiting families stand apart?

Egalitarian families

Research in other countries where marriage remains the norm suggests that cohabiting couples may be more egalitarian than married couples. Unmarried American couples, for example, were found to be less traditional than married couples in their attitudes towards gender roles, although not markedly different in the actual division of household labour between partners.[11] Similar findings have been reported for Australia, where a study carried out in the late 1970s found that cohabiting couples were less traditional in the division of household tasks between partners than were married couples.[12] Here in Britain, it appears that among all couples, attitudes are changing more quickly than behaviour, and that women continue to assume primary responsibility for childcare and housework and to carry out most routine household tasks, even when employed.[13]

In order to gain some understanding of any differences in household organisation between long-term cohabiting couples and married couples, we investigated a range of behaviours and attitudes, including money management and financial decision-making; actual and preferred responsibility for housework, providing an income, childcare and managing money; and the domestic division of labour. Generally, few significant differences existed between our four mains groups of women. If any tendency could be identified at all, it was *not* that cohabiting couples were more egalitarian than married couples, but that married women who did not live with their husbands outside marriage tended to be *less* egalitarian (or more traditional) than women who did cohabit – whether or not the latter ultimately married.

Because our findings were consistently in the direction of 'no significant difference' (and thus highly repetitive), we restrict our presentation to selected key attributes of family organisation. Table 6.4 summarises four measures of egalitarian attitudes, while Tables 6.5 and 6.6

Table 6.4   Four measures of egalitarian attitudes, according to living arrangements

Column percentages

| | Long-term cohabiting mothers | Cohabited pre-maritally | | Non-cohab. married mothers |
		Married after baby	Married before baby	
(1) How are most important decisions made?				
Partners have equal say	73	73	77	76
(2) Who has final say in big financial decisions?				
Partners have equal say	66	75	63	63
(3) Who *does have* responsibility for ensuring adequate family income?				
Both partners	27	39	33	23
Male partner	62	55	56	74
(4) Who *should have* responsibility for ensuring adequate family income?				
Both partners	55	67	56	52
Male partner	38	29	40	44
Base:	*77*	*51*	*57*	*92*

indicate the domestic division of labour among cohabiting and married couples.

The views that are summarised in Table 6.4 were derived largely from a self-completion questionnaire, filled in by respondents at various times during their interviews. In recording their answers, women were invited to choose between 'male partner', 'female partner', 'both equally', or 'don't know'.[14] For ease of presentation, only a part of each set of possible responses are included in Table 6.4.

Household decision-making
The first panel in Table 6.4 relates to household decision-making, and illustrates the general tendency for women's views to converge across

different living arrangements. About three-quarters of each group of women we interviewed reported that both partners had an equal say in important decisions in their households. Taking women's current employment status into account had no impact on the views of non-cohabiting married women, but altered the proportions reporting joint decision-making among women with some experience of cohabitation.

For example, overall 73 per cent of both long-term cohabiting mothers and women who married *after* having children reported that decision-making in their households was joint; *employed* women in these two groups were *less* likely to give this response than women who were not currently in paid work. For mothers who were *continuing* to cohabit, the differences were marked: 64 per cent of employed cohabiting mothers reported that important decisions were made jointly, compared with 80 per cent of non-working cohabiting mothers.

The impact of employment status on the responses of cohabiting women who married *before* having children provided a mirror-image contrast to the views of still-cohabiting mothers. Overall, 77 per cent of cohabiting women who married *before* having children reported joint decision-making, rising to 86 per cent of among employed women in this group and falling to 68 per cent of the non-employed. A brief reflection on the social and economic circumstances of these two groups of women may explain, in part at least, the differing impact of employment status on decision-making in their households.

Among all women with partners/husbands, long-term cohabiting mothers were the least likely to be currently employed (43 per cent) and included the largest proportion living in households where no one was employed (23 per cent). It seems plausible at least that mutual unemployment might encourage joint decision-making among partners, if only to share the burden. In contrast, over half of the women who married *before* having children were currently employed – and over half of these employed women held professional or managerial jobs. In just over one-quarter (26 per cent) of their households, both husband and wife held service class jobs. It seems likely that women who are used to exercising authority or expertise at work would expect to do so at home as well. Their apparent relinquishment of joint responsibility for decisions when out of the labour market might well reflect the resultant marked disparity in resources between themselves and their professionally-employed husbands.

Important financial decisions

The second panel of Table 6.4 focuses directly on financial decision-making and reflects women's responses to a question asking who had the final say in big financial decisions. Again, the tendency was for women's views to converge across different living arrangements, although in this instance, cohabiting women who married *after* having children stood out. As might be expected, women's employment status had the same general impact as discussed above; but the greatest change came in relation to cohabiting women who married *after* having children.

Overall, 75 per cent of cohabiting women who married *after* becoming mothers reported joint final say in financial decisions, rising to 79 per cent among currently employed women, and falling to 68 per cent among non-employed women. In the three other groups of women, being out of the labour market tended to increase slightly their chances of equality in big financial decisions. Again, it seems reasonable to look to women's employment characteristics to explain the impact of being currently employed. Cohabiting women who married *after* having children were the most likely of all women to be employed (57 per cent); 1 in 5 worked currently in professional or managerial jobs. They were also the least likely to be unqualified and the most likely to be educated to degree level. From these characteristics, what seems to be in need of explanation is not why being currently employed increased the participation of these women in major financial decisions, but why it seemed not to do so with respect to household decision-making generally.[15]

Being the breadwinner

The last two panels in Table 6.4 summarise women's views about which partner had ultimate responsibility for ensuring an adequate family income and which partner should have had such responsibility. The majority of women in each group reported that actual responsibility rested with her partner or husband; only a small minority reported that they personally carried this responsibility. Among married women, however, those who had not lived with their husbands before marriage were substantially more likely than those who did cohabit to depend upon their husbands for financial support. Almost three-quarters of non-cohabiting married women reported that their husbands had ultimate responsibility for providing an adequate family income, compared with just over half of women who had cohabited before marriage. Bringing women's employment status into account had an expected effect: consistently higher proportions of women who were not currently in work reported that their husbands or partners assumed the breadwinner's responsibilities.

The last panel in Table 6.4 indicates which partner women thought *should have* responsibility for providing an adequate income for the family, and provides an interesting contrast with actual practice. In each group the proportion of women who cited both partners equally rose substantially; and, indeed, doubled in the case of still-cohabiting mothers and women who had never cohabited. The views of the currently employed were more markedly in the direction of shared responsibility than the views of women who were not in the labour force.

The tendency for non-cohabiting married women to be more traditional in attitudes and behaviour than women with some experience of cohabitation became evident as our analyses focused on which partner carried (or should carry) responsibility for various aspects of family life. The last two panels of Table 6.4 provide a first indication in relation to ensuring an adequate family income. Women who did not live with their husbands before marriage were substantially more likely than other women to report that their husbands had actual responsibility as breadwinners; they were also more likely to report that their husbands should have such responsibility. Indeed, *employed* non-cohabiting women were the most likely among working women to say that husbands should have breadwinner responsibility and the least likely to say that such responsibility should be shared. To juxtapose the two extremes in lifestyle: 27 per cent of *continuing* to cohabit women currently in work suggested that men ought to have ultimate responsibility for ensuring the family's income; but 41 per cent of employed women who did not live with their husbands before marriage felt this way. In relation to shared responsibility, the proportions were, respectively, 70 per cent and 57 per cent.

Non-cohabiting married women also were more likely to report that their husbands had ultimate responsibility – and should have ultimate responsibility – for organising the household money and paying bills, while they were responsible – and should be responsible – for ensuring that the housework was done properly. Typically female household tasks, those that need to be done everyday, appeared to be the particular domain of non-cohabiting married women, whose reports about who did what in the household tended to differ from those of women with some experience of cohabitation.

The domestic division of labour
Tables 6.5 and 6.6 summarise the proportions in each group of women who reported that a range of household tasks were shared equally or done entirely or mainly by themselves.[16] In each table, three types of information about the domestic division of labour is provided. First, the tables

Table 6.5   Household division of labour (I): Proportion who reported tasks shared equally

Column percentages

	Long-term cohabiting mothers	Cohabited pre-maritally		Non-cohab. married mothers
		Married after baby	Married before baby	
*Cleaning	22	18	14	7
*Washing up	34	33	35	29
*Cooking	20	29	27	14
*Washing clothes	12	6	4	1
Taking children to doctor	31	26	28	34
Painting/decorating	26	31	25	34
Car maintenance	8	14	10	5
Gardening	48	48	46	39
Helping children with homework	60	47	62	61
Base:	*77*	*51*	*57*	*92*
"Mean score"	2.31	2.31	2.30	2.10

One way analysis of variance:
    d.f. = 3   p < 0.7 (not significant)

*Four task analysis
"Mean score"	.87	.84	.81	.51

    d.f. = 3   p < 0.04

summarise the percentage distributions of 9 household tasks across women with different marital and cohabitation histories. Secondly, a 'mean score' is given for each group of women, indicating the average number of tasks that were either shared or primarily done by women. The closer each score comes to 9, the more household tasks were shared (done primarily by women). Thirdly, results of significance tests are provided for tables which included all 9 tasks and for only 4, typically female, tasks. These four tasks were cleaning the house, washing up, cooking for the family and washing clothes.

Table 6.6   Household division of labour (II): Proportion who reported tasks done entirely or mainly by women

Column percentages

	Long-term cohabiting mothers	Cohabited pre-maritally		Non-cohab. married mothers
		Married after baby	Married before baby	
*Cleaning	77	74	81	90
*Washing up	57	50	51	60
*Cooking	75	63	72	84
*Washing clothes	87	94	96	97
Taking children to doctor	65	74	70	64
Painting/decorating	13	28	19	12
Car maintenance	5	11	4	4
Gardening	23	29	25	22
Helping children with homework	40	43	36	33
Base:	*77*	*51*	*56*	*92*
"Mean score"	4.25	4.55	4.40	4.59

One way analysis of variance:
    d.f. = 3   p < 0.6 (not significant)

*Four task analysis

"Mean score"	2.96	2.84	2.98	3.30

    d.f. = 3   p < 0.04

The information provided by percentage distributions is ample, but the least amenable to interpretation. For example, it is not clear what to make of the fact that cohabiting women who married *after* having children were the most likely to share cooking and car maintenance, but the least likely to have partners who equally helped their children with homework. Or that washing clothes was the least likely to be done entirely or mainly by still-cohabiting mothers, and cleaning the house most likely to be done by non-cohabiting married women.

However, the mean scores provided in each table in relation to all 9 tasks suggest that overall, few differences existed between women with differing marital and cohabitation histories. Just over 2 tasks were shared equally between partners according to the reports of women in each group; and just over 4 tasks were done entirely or mainly by women, whatever their current living arrangements. Moreover, significance tests based on all 9 tasks confirmed the essential sameness of overall household organisation suggested by the mean scores.

If, however, we restrict our attention to the 4 tasks shown in Tables 6.5 and 6.6 that are constant, almost daily, features of family life – particularly when there are young children around – then differences of some interest are revealed. Specifically, women who did not live with their husbands before marriage were less likely to report that their partners shared with them cooking, cleaning, laundry and washing up; and the most likely to report that these tasks were done entirely or mainly by themselves. This picture of domestic organisation, encapsulated by the mean scores shown in each table, was confirmed statistically.

Thus it was the case that our findings revealed differences of interest in the family lives of women with different marital and cohabitation histories. But it was women who did not live with their husbands outside marriage who stood apart, rather than those who were *continuing* to cohabit many years after becoming mothers. The difference between non-cohabiting women and those who (ever) cohabited was in an expected direction: women who chose to marry straight away tended to be more traditional in both attitudes and behaviour, inclinations which remained essentially unchanged when current employment status was taken into account. While this may not be particularly surprising, the fact that long-term cohabiting couples differed so little from cohabiting couples who ultimately married is of rather more interest.

From our account of family life, long-term cohabiting couples are not noticeably more egalitarian in beliefs than other couples with some experience of cohabitation, nor are they particularly more likely to share daily household chores. They show no distinctive pattern of financial or household decision-making. They are, in these respects at least, generally indistinguishable from other couples who had lived together outside marriage for some period.[17]

We would wish to emphasise, however, that all of the couples represented here had children. It is recognised that egalitarian behaviour between couples often evaporates with the birth of their first child. Kiernan's and Estaugh's work on cohabitation and extra-marital childbearing, for example, shows that childless cohabiting couples under age 35 were more likely to state that domestic tasks were shared (34 per cent) than childless married couples (24 per cent) in the same age group. However, the proportions reporting shared domestic tasks among both cohabiting and married couples dropped to 1 in 10 when only couples with children were considered.[18]

Explaining a lack of difference is always difficult. It may be that the majority of couples are now drifting closer towards egalitarian attitudes and behaviour, just as the majority now live together before getting married. The breaking down of rigid, prescriptive rules about marriage may also entail the breaking down of gender roles (and rules) within marriage – although our study only provides scant evidence of this, and that little is negative.

It may be that social class or ethnic background is more important for household organisation than one's marital or cohabitation history. Because of respondent numbers, we could not explore the impact of ethnicity; while in class terms, we can report that no consistent differences were found by social class of respondent, partner or respondent's family background. Superficially, one might have expected this: the large majority of *continuing* to cohabit women were working-class, while most cohabiting women who ultimately married were middle-class, by their own or partner's occupation if not in family background. And yet, the views of these three groups of women were markedly similar, at least in regard to decision-making, who did what in their households and who should.

Sharing good times and bad

Two further aspects of our exploration of cohabiting family life concerned the extent to which still-cohabiting couples spent their leisure time together and the extent to which women in long-term cohabiting unions shared their problems with their partners. *A priori* it seemed possible to build arguments either way: cohabiting couples would spend more time together than other couples, and share their problems more frequently, because they would recognise a need to reaffirm their willingness to be together:

> Living together I think you try harder. You don't take one another for granted so much as if we were married. You keep trying to stay together more. I reckon you work harder at the relationship than if you are married. 157/3688

> We stay together more. [...] we make more of an effort to stay together. 234/5531

> You don't take each other for granted as much. I don't know really, I don't know how to describe it. I suppose you have to work harder at it, the relationship. I don't know, it is just everything in general. 037/2070

Conversely, cohabiting couples might lead very separate lives, sharing a home and child, but little else:

You have no ties to each other – he does his thing, I do mine. 205/1963

He has his money and I have mine, which suits us both [...] I can still live my own life and be my own person. 084/0133

He thinks he can do as he pleases. He can go out while I look after the children. 245/4916

After the evidence was collected, of course, cohabiting couples turned out to be not very different from other couples.

Table 6.7 summarises the extent to which women reported that they shared outside interests with their partners or husbands. Just over half in each group of women reported that they shared all or some leisure interests with their partners and about one-third reported that they shared a few such activities. Differences existed in relation to the proportions who reported that they shared no outside interests with their partners, but these formed no particular pattern.

Table 6.7   Proportion who reported shared leisure activities, according to living arrangements

Column percentages

| | Long-term cohabiting mothers | Cohabited pre-maritally | | Non-cohab. married mothers |
		Married after baby	Married before baby	
All shared	13	6	5	4
Some shared	38	49	46	49
A few shared	33	35	30	36
None shared	12	8	18	9
No answer	5	2	2	2
Base:	*77*	*51*	*57*	*92*

Table 6.7 represents women's responses to a question included in the self-completion questionnaire which was filled in at various times during their interviews. In addition, interviewers asked women whether they engaged in a range of spare time activities, and with whom they did these activities. Women were asked how often over the course of one month they had done each of 19 separate activities, ranging from swimming to watching television to attending leisure groups such as yoga or art classes.

For purposes of analyses, 5 activities not strictly defined as leisure were eliminated and the frequency of activity collapsed into having done the activity at all during the last month versus not having done it at all.[19] In

Table 6.8   'Mean leisure scores' by living arrangements

	Long-term cohabiting mothers	Cohabited pre-maritally		Non-cohab. married mothers
		Married after baby	Married before baby	
Leisure activities as:				
A couple	1.29	1.73	1.34	1.59
d.f. = 3	p < 0.2 (n.s.)			
A family	2.61	2.88	3.09	3.09
d.f. = 3	p <0.3 (n.s.)			
A mother	2.01	1.84	1.93	1.89
d.f. = 3	p <0.9 (n.s.)			
An individual	2.06	2.12	1.77	1.98
d.f. = 3	p < 0.6 (n.s.)			
Base:	*77*	*51*	*57*	*92*

addition, four 'companion' categories were devised to cover activities engaged in (1) as a couple, including the respondent and her partner or husband only; (2) as a family, including the respondent, her partner and children; (3) as a mother, including the respondent and her children only; and (4) as an individual, including the respondent alone or with work colleagues, neighbours, friends or relatives other than her partner and children.

In the event, no significant differences between couples with differing marital and cohabitation histories were uncovered by our analyses, although there appeared to be a *tendency* for still-cohabiting mothers to engage in fewer activities as part of a couple or family and in more activities as a mother or individual. Table 6.8 summarises the 'mean activity score' for each group (out of 14 activities) and indicates the significance level.

Counting leisure activities as 'good times', we also asked cohabiting mothers about the 'bad times' and whether they shared their problems with their partners. This time we had no *a priori* expectations. Table 6.9 summarises our findings.

As indicated, long-term cohabiting mothers were not noticeably different from other mothers in the extent to which they confided in their

Table 6.9 Proportion who reported sharing problems with partner/husband

Column percentages

	Long-term cohabiting mothers	Cohabited pre-maritally Married after baby	Married before baby	Non-cohab. married mothers
Shares...				
All problems	35	31	40	37
Most problems	39	35	35	45
Some problems	10	29	16	16
None/hardly any	10	2	7	1
No answer	5	2	2	1
Base:	*77*	*51*	*57*	*92*

partners. It is interesting to note that women who did not live with their husbands before getting married were the most likely to report that they shared all or most of their problems with their husbands (82 per cent); and that cohabiting women who married *after* having children were the least likely to do so (66 per cent). There were no differences between the remaining two groups of women, among whom three-quarters reported sharing all or most of their problems.

It is likely to be of further interest that women who were married for the second time (or cohabiting after a previous marriage) were more likely to report that they shared all or most of their problems with their partners than were women married for the first time. This association was least strong among still-cohabiting women; and held among married women even when it was their husband who had been married before. However, while this result seems inherently plausible, it is based on a small number of respondents in each group and therefore needs to be treated with caution.[20]

But are they happy?
Finally, we attempted to answer the question, are long-term cohabiting mothers as happy or happier than other mothers? Accordingly, we first asked women a direct question: how happy is your relationship, all things considered? In response, women were invited to tick one of 7 boxes ranging from extremely happy through neither happy nor unhappy to extremely unhappy. Women were then asked to indicate the extent to which they

agreed or disagreed with their partners across 11 aspects of family life. This was followed by a question about whether women had ever wished they had not married or cohabited; and lastly, if women had their lives to live over again, whether they would live with or marry the same partner again, whether they would choose a new partner, or remain unattached. Each of these questions was included in the self-completion questionnaire.

Table 6.10 summarises the extent to which women reported that they and their partner nearly always or often agreed about various aspects of family and social life. Before commenting on the results shown, it is worth noting that there was an unusually high level of non-response among two groups of women: those who were *continuing* to cohabit, of whom about 7 per cent consistently did not answer; and cohabiting women who had married *before* having children, of whom about 10 per cent did not answer. The level of non-response among the remaining two groups hovered between 2 to 4 per cent. We are unable explain why a disproportionate number of women from two groups would decline to answer these particular questions: one would expect questionnaire 'fatigue' or problems with understanding to apply across each group rather than be concentrated in this way. However, it seems worth bearing the level of non-response in mind, together with the fact that women also were offered the option of reporting that they had never discussed the particular issue with their partners.

The results presented in Table 6.10 are divided into three parts, as before. First, the various percentage distributions are shown for each group of women in relation to the extent of agreement between themselves and their partners. Secondly, 'mean agreement scores' are given for each group, together with the results of significance testing. Finally, 'mean disagreement scores' and overall significance level are given for each group. No percentage distributions in relation to the extent of disagreement are included as they added little to the general picture. We do, however, comment on some 'disagreement' differences in the text.

Our intent in compiling Table 6.10 was to gain an overall sense of how much (or how little) the women we interviewed and their husbands or partners agreed on fairly basic aspects of family and social life. Once compiled, however, the table does not lend itself to ease of interpretation. For example, cohabiting women who married *after* having children were considerably less likely than other women to agree with their partner's outlook on life, but rather more likely to agree with him about showing affection for each other and having sex together. Cohabiting women who married *before* having children agreed less with their partners about relations with their parents and parents-in-law. Women who did not cohabit before marriage seemed in particular agreement with their husbands about deciding when or if to have children. Long-term cohabiting women were 4 times more likely than never-cohabiting women to disagree with their partners about liking the same friends. And about 1 in 6 women in each group disagreed with their partners about sharing household tasks.

Given the focus of our research, about the most definite comment that can be made from these findings is that there seems to be nothing particularly distinctive about long-term cohabiting mothers and the extent to which they agreed or disagreed with their partners. A glance at the 'mean agreement scores' appears to confirm this view; which, if anything, suggest a slight tendency for non-cohabiting married couples to agree more often on basic issues of family and social life than couples with histories which

Table 6.10 Proportions who reported agreement between partners on 11 aspects of family life, according to living arrangements

Column percentages

	Long-term cohabiting mothers	Cohabited pre-maritally		Non-cohab. married mothers
		Married after baby	Married before baby	
Handling finances	59	67	58	65
Spare time	62	52	58	62
Showing affection	60	74	62	64
Having sex	51	71	58	68
Liking same friends	49	55	49	66
Outlook on life	56	46	64	62
Behaving decently	66	66	68	74
Sharing household tasks	47	47	43	53
Relations with parents/ in-laws	55	61	44	56
When to have children	64	61	70	81
How children brought up	61	61	69	73
Base:	*77*	*51*	*57*	*92*
"Mean score"	6.29	6.57	6.40	7.23
d.f = 3 p <0.2 (n.s.)				
"Mean disagreement score"	.81	.61	.70	.67
d.f. = 3 p < 0.9 (n.s.)				

include cohabitation. However, the differences shown between groups are not statistically significant.

A rather more interesting view of long-term cohabiting mothers is presented in Table 6.11. We asked women to indicate whether they had ever wished they had not married or cohabited. No reference was made to their current partner or husband, and 4 possible answers were provided. The results of this line of questioning are presented in the top panel of Table 6.11. However, we also asked women to indicate whether, given the chance to live life over again, they would choose the same partner, a different partner, or not to marry or cohabit at all. We also gave women the opportunity to indicate that they did not know what they would do in these circumstances. These results are summarised in the bottom panel of Table 6.11.

Table 6.11 Two measures of relationship stability

Column percentages

	Long-term cohabiting mothers	Cohabited pre-maritally Married after baby	Married before baby	Non-cohab. married mothers
A If respondent has ever wished she had not married or cohabited				
Frequently	3	6	4	5
Occasionally	16	10	9	11
Only rarely	30	39	42	32
No	46	43	44	50
No answer	7	2	2	2
B If respondent could live her life over again, she would...				
Choose same partner	56	75	75	78
Choose different partner	0	2	4	7
Not marry or cohabit	5	6	7	2
Don't know	39	18	14	13
No answer	0	0	0	0
Base:	*77*	*51*	*57*	*92*

If we restrict our attention to the top panel of the table, *continuing* to cohabit women do not appear particularly distinctive. They were marginally more likely to report that they had frequently or occasionally wished they had not cohabited, and marginally less likely to report that they had had these thoughts only rarely. But these differences were slight indeed, and long-term cohabiting mothers – whether married previously or not – appeared no more or less likely in general to wish that they had not cohabited.

However, if we direct our attention to the bottom panel of the table, a different picture emerges, and one which suggests a degree of instability in cohabiting relationships that is not found in marriage. When asked whom they would choose if given the chance to live their lives again, three-quarters or more married women reported that they would choose their current husband. Long-term cohabiting mothers, in contrast, were much more uncertain about their choice: while just over half (56 per cent) said that they would live with the same partner again, 39 per cent said that they did not know what they would do.

Closer examination of these results in relation to cohabiting mothers' previous marital history revealed that it was largely the never-marrieds who were uncertain: among still-cohabiting women who had not been legally married before cohabiting with their current partner, 44 per cent reported that they did not know what they would do if given the chance to live their lives over and only a bare half (51 per cent) would choose to live with the same partner. Still-cohabiting mothers who had been married before were much more like married mothers, and 13 out of 18 reported that they would choose to live with the same partner. Having been married before also increased the chances that married women would choose to marry the same husband, but only by one or two percentage points.

Of course, being uncertain about what one might do in a hypothetical 'second chance' existence – or even being certain that one would choose a different partner – does not mean that separation or cohabitation breakdown is imminent. Indeed, if the results presented in Table 6.12 are to be believed, the bottom panel of Table 6.11 tells us very little. Table 6.12 summarises women's responses to a question which asked them how happy their relationship with their husband or partner was, all things considered. Neither the percentage distribution of women through the 7-point scale nor the 'mean happiness scores' presented in Table 6.12 suggest the existence of important differences in women's estimations of their relationships, and the results proved to be not significant.

However, an observant reader will note the similar 'mean happiness scores' achieved by *continuing* to cohabit women and those who married *before* having children. (It might also be noted that the higher the score, out of 7, the unhappier the respondent.) And yet, these two groups of women returned markedly different responses to our enquiries about their actions in a 'second chance' world, at least when the small number of previously-married women were disregarded. Over three quarters of one

Table 6.12 Happiness scores, according to living arrangements

Column percentages

	Long-term cohabiting mothers	Cohabited pre-maritally Married after baby	Married before baby	Non-cohab. married mothers
1. Extremely happy	54	55	50	56
2.	20	22	21	21
3.	9	12	16	7
4. Neither happy nor unhappy	11	10	7	13
5.	4	0	2	2
6.	0	2	2	0
7. Extremely unhappy	3	0	2	1
Base:	*76*	*51*	*56*	*90*
"Mean score"	2.01	1.84	2.02	1.90

d.f. = 3 $p < 0.9$ (n.s.)

group would choose the same partner; almost one half of the other group did not know who or what they would choose. But both were about equally happy (whether or not they had been married before).

Thus, it would seem that our one indication of potential instability among cohabiting relationships, based on the choices cohabiting mothers might make in a different life, is generally unsupported by the rest of our analyses. The family lives of cohabiting mothers are not so very different from the lives of married mothers: such women are as likely or unlikely to share household tasks, leisure and problems; they are as likely or unlikely to share their partner's views on a range of social and family issues; they are as happy or unhappy as other mothers. And yet, the results presented in Table 6.11 cannot but intrigue one's attention: *why would only 1 in 2 cohabiting mothers choose the same partner if given a second chance at life?*

Notes

1. Jacqueline Priest, *Families Outside Marriage*, Family Law/Jordan and Sons, Bristol, 1990. p.135.
2. Priest, Ibid, pp 188-9. During the latter half of this century, the legal position of children born and reared outside wedlock has improved considerably, particularly in relation to inheritance. The 1969 Family Law Reform Act established the same right of a child born outside marriage as one born within marriage to receive gifts

by will, and the right to inherit on the intestacy of either parent (but not of grandparents or siblings). Children born outside marriage were also given the right to claim maintenance from a deceased parent's estate. See Kiernan and Estaugh (1993) for a detailed discussion of the legal rights of children born to unmarried couples; and also, S.M. Cretney and J.M. Masson, *Principles of Family Law, 5th Edition*, Sweet and Maxwell, London, 1990.

3.   One area that remains unexplored by our study concerns steps cohabitants may take to provide for each other financially, particularly in the event of cohabitation breakdown or of a partner's death. Unmarried couples have few legal rights or obligations towards each other, either during their lifetimes or after death. Cohabitants have no legal duty to support each other while living together; unless named as a beneficiary, an unmarried partner has no automatic right to provision from a deceased partner's estate. Financially dependent cohabitants may make application for provision under the Inheritance (Provision for Family and Dependents) Act 1975, but if there is a surviving spouse, that spouse may be able to bring a successful claim on the entire estate. Moreover, if both partners were self-supporting financially and contributed jointly to the household, the surviving partner cannot make a claim against the deceased's estate; nor can a claim be made by a surviving partner who was the sole earner. Clearly this area merits exploration; although our results in relation to children do not encourage us to suppose that many cohabiting couples will have taken the necessary steps to protect each other financially (see below in the text). See Kiernan and Estaugh (1993) for an informed discussion of the legal consequences of cohabitation for partners. See also J. Bowler, J. Jackson and E. Loughridge, *Living Together: You, Your Partner and the Law*, Century, London, 1991.

4.   Priest, op.cit., pp 155-6.

5.   A child born to unmarried parents who later marry is said to have been *legitimated*. Since the 1976 Legitimacy Act, children born to married parents (legitimate) and to unmarried parents who subsequently marry (legitimated) have been considered equal in terms of support, inheritance and claims for damages and compensation.

6.   Chapter 7 examines the circumstances of 32 women who had experienced the breakdown of their cohabiting relationship. One part of this analysis is concerned with the establishment of a legal relationship between father and child.

7.   See note 2; our understanding of family law suggests that at least the child mentioned in the quote following should have been able to benefit from his/her father's estate, even if his/her mother was not entitled to do so.

8.   It is becoming increasingly difficult to maintain a legal dichotomy between married and unmarried couples. Parker argues that there has been a 'gradual and halting' juridification of some kinds of cohabiting relationships (namely, those whose incumbents behave like married people), to the extent that the State is slowly admitting cohabitation as an informal marriage status. Parker, op.cit., pp.96-97 and 127. See also our concluding discussion in Chapter 8.

9.   Married women who did not live with their husbands prior to marriage were not asked about the names used by themselves or their children.

10. When we asked respondents about the family names used by themselves, partners and children, we were interested primarily in the extent to which the same name was or was not used by all family members. We did not explicitly ask respondents if using different names caused problems; the information about this that we

received arose spontaneously in response to questions about the disadvantages of cohabitation, the impact of cohabitation on children and whether respondents ever felt pressured to marry. It seems likely that had we addressed the issue more directly, further evidence of difficulties caused by differing family names would have emerged.

11. Risman, et al, op.cit., 1981, pp.77-83; Stafford, et al, op.cit., 1977, pp.43-57.

12 Cunningham, and Anthill, op.cit., 1979.

13. K.E.Kiernan, 'The roles of men and women in tomorrow's Europe', *Employment Gazette*, October 1992; J. Gershuny, 'Change in the domestic division of labour in the UK, 1975-1987: dependent labour versus adaptive partnership', in N. Abercrombie and A. Warde (eds) *Social Change in Contemporary Britain*, Polity Press, Cambridge, 1982.

14. Exceptionally, the question about final say in financial decisions was included in the main questionnaire and thus asked by the interviewer. Also, respondents were offered a further choice in relation to important household decisions: male (female) partner has a lot more say; has somewhat more say.

15. It was the case, however, that cohabiting women who married *after* having children were substantially less likely than other women to accord either themselves or their partners 'a lot more say' in important decisions (none did so) and hence more likely to appear to be leaning towards equality. This is an area which, like others, seems worth more detailed research.

16. The tables are derived from self-completion questions. The full range of choices offered to respondents was: female partner almost entirely, female partner mainly, both equally, male partner mainly, male partner almost entirely, neither of us do this, not applicable.

17. Our findings also suggest that cohabiting fathers are no more or less likely to spend time with their children than other fathers.

18. Kiernan and Estaugh, op.cit., Chapter 2. For these analyses, the authors used 1989 Social Attitudes survey data.

19. The 5 non-leisure activities eliminated were attending an act of worship, evening study classes or a political meeting, doing unpaid voluntary work, and doing other unpaid work for people outside the household.

20. Number of women married previously among:
Continuing to cohabit mothers = 18
Married *after* baby born = 14
Married *before* baby born = 11
Did not cohabit = 4

7   Cohabitation breakdown

Cohabitation tends towards instability, ending in either marriage or dissolution. One recent analysis suggests that fewer than 1 in 5 cohabiting women live with their partners for more than 5 years, with 54 per cent cohabiting for two years or less.[1] About half of the women we contacted for interviews had been known to be cohabiting some 4 years earlier. When interviewed in 1993, 32 of these 166 women were found to have separated from those partners, including 10 who had formed new partnerships.

In this chapter, we focus on the consequences of cohabitation breakdown for the children born to cohabiting parents; specifically, on the relationship – if any – between the 4 year old children born during cohabitation and their now absent fathers. Thus, we examine whether unmarried absent fathers had taken any legal responsibility for their children, whether they contributed financially to their care and whether contact between father and child had been maintained. In addition, we look briefly at the role *cohabiting* might have played in the breakdown of relationships.

Cohabitation breakdown and poverty

For the majority of the women we interviewed, cohabitation breakdown meant entry into lone parenthood and poverty. Over 1 in 5 British families with dependent children are headed by a lone parent. Until recently, lone parent families came into existence largely as a result of *marriage* breakdown. Today however, changing patterns of marriage and motherhood mean that cohabitation breakdown is an increasingly frequent route into lone parenthood. Bradshaw and Millar, for example, estimated that in 1990 about one-fifth of never-married lone mothers had been cohabiting before they became lone parents.[2]

Never-married lone mothers are the most rapidly growing group within lone parents and represent, moreover, the most rapidly growing group of lone parents on state benefits.[3] Seven out of ten lone parents are dependent on income support, almost twice as many as in 1971.[4] The number of lone mothers on long term benefits doubled during the 1980s; estimates suggest that over 60 per cent of lone mother families are poor compared with only 20 per cent of two parent families.[5]

The formerly-cohabiting women we interviewed reflected the generally high level of dependency on state benefits among lone mothers. When interviewed, 66 per cent were in receipt of income support, a benefit which is paid to families who have no main wage earner. Thirty-one per cent had received family credit (an income related benefit for employed parents) at some time during the previous three years; 16 per cent were receiving family credit at the time of interviews in June/July 1993.

With an average age of 27 years, formerly-cohabiting mothers were thus among the youngest, and the poorest, of the women we interviewed. Sixty per cent were not in employment when contacted for interviews: about one-third had not worked since the birth of their four year old child; 1 in 5 had not worked either before or since that birth. Largely from working-class family backgrounds, 59 per cent lived in local council housing, while 74 per cent had annual incomes of £6,000 or less, reflecting their dependency on state benefits. Only 10 per cent received any financial support for themselves from their former partners, although half received some support for their children. (For a comparison of these characteristics with women who were continuing to cohabit, see Table 3.1).

Father and child

The findings we report here about unmarried absent fathers and their children do not take into account 3 women whose cohabitation relationships had broken down. During their interviews, these 3 women indicated that the partner with whom each had been living shortly after the birth of her 4 year old child was not that child's father.[6] In this situation, interviewers were instructed not to ask respondents about the legal relationship and maintenance of contact between her former partner and her child, nor about any financial contributions to the child's care made by her former partner. We accept, however, that in some cases, such relationships might have been established between man and child, despite the absence of a biological tie.

All but one of the 29 remaining women reported that mother and father had jointly registered their child's birth. The exception involved a child born in Ireland, where joint registrations by unmarried parents are difficult. Furthermore, two-thirds of these children carried their father's family name, either alone (52 per cent) or in tandem with their mother's family name (15 per cent). From these findings, it seems likely that some expectation of permanence had been attached to the relationship between the cohabiting couple, prior to its breakdown.

Table 7.1 **Cohabitation breakdown: reasons why no legal relationship**
established between father and child

	Column percentages
Never thought about it	26
Considered it unnecessary	31
Father is 'real' father	7
Birth registered by father	7
Thought it was automatic	7
Child/father have good relations	7
Just not necessary	3
Other reasons	24
Prefer informality	3
Haven't got around to it yet	3
Partner rejected responsibility	14
Doesn't want to see partner	3
No reason given	9
Legal relationship established	10
Base: formerly cohabiting women	29

As we outlined in the last chapter, however, the fathers of children born to unmarried couples have no automatic parental rights, and joint registration of a child's birth does not confer those rights. In that chapter, moreover, we reported that none of the women who were *continuing* to cohabit had taken steps to establish a legal relationship between their partner and child; nor, prior to marrying, had any of the cohabiting women who married *after* having children. Indeed, our findings suggest that cohabiting mothers generally are unaware that specific steps need to be taken in order to establish such a formal, legal tie between father and child.

Ignorance of the law also existed among women whose cohabitation had ended in breakdown, and almost 1 in 3 reported that no legal steps had been taken because they had believed that such action was unnecessary. One in 10 women, however, had gone to court with the father to establish his parental rights: 1 couple during the time they were continuing to cohabit, and 2 others after the breakdown of the relationship. Table 7.1 summarises the reports of formerly-cohabiting mothers about why no legal relationship was established between father and child either before or after cohabitation breakdown.

The reasons given by women whose cohabitation had ended generally mirrored those reported by women who were *continuing* to cohabit (see Table 6.2), with an obvious exception: reasons explicitly connected with the ending of their relationships. Four formerly-cohabiting women reported that no legal relationship had been established between father and child because the father had abandoned, or refused to take, any responsibility for his child. One further woman indicated that it was her decision that there would be no contact between father and child:

> No. No. He doesn't see him, he's not interested. That's all there is to say on the matter, he's not interested. 071/2055

> I don't want anything to do with him. 082/4728

But these 5 women apart, the reasons given for not establishing a legal relationship between father and child were those we met in the last chapter: I didn't know; It wasn't necessary; There was no need.

> No, there was just no need. When he was living here he was just like a dad. We used to go out together and take our daughter with us. I didn't think there was any need. I just didn't think we'd ever split up. 102/4464

> Like I have explained my daughter's father and myself are good friends. We think it's only another expense to do anything legal. He sees my daughter every week and helps when he can. It's just that we find we can't live together anymore but are good friends. 287/6276

> I didn't know anything about it. I thought it was alright because he was registered on the birth certificate. 117/4329

Financial support

Three women whose cohabitation had ended had gone to the courts with the father in order to establish his parental rights. Two of these women, together with a third woman, additionally had a formal agreement with their former partners under which they received maintenance payments. Two others had written wills naming their former partners as guardian to their children. But by far the most common agreement between formerly-cohabiting partners concerned child support payments.

Half of the women we interviewed whose cohabitation had broken down reported that their former partners contributed financially to the care and support of their 4 year old child.[7] Of these 14 women, 9 reported that they had a formal, legal arrangement with their former partners concerning child support, while the remaining 5 women indicated that their former partner contributed financially on an informal basis. Generally, where child support payments were made, few problems appeared to arise and most women expressed satisfaction with the financial arrangements that they had made with their former partners. However, 2 women reported that such payments were often late, while 3 others suggested that they would like to receive more money. Eight of the 14 women who received no child support expressed dissatisfaction with this arrangement.

Contact between father and child

The large majority of unmarried absent fathers maintained contact with their children. Seventeen fathers (out of 28, see note 7) saw their sons or daughters at least once a week, 2 were in contact at least once a fortnight, while 3 restricted their visits to monthly or less frequent ones.

Somewhat surprisingly, perhaps, establishing a formal, legal relationship between father and child did not appear to guarantee that contact would be maintained: 1 out of the 3 women who had been to court with the father to establish his parental rights reported that her former partner did not see his child (although he contributed financially to the child's care). However, physical proximity did appear to encourage contact: 15 out of the 22 fathers who regularly saw their children lived either within walking distance or in the same village or town. The 7 remaining fathers all lived in the same county.

We can say little about the reasons unmarried absent fathers lose contact with their children, as we have the reports of only 6 formerly-cohabiting mothers on the matter. Their reports are highly suggestive, however, of the lack of commitment to fatherhood that *may* accompany cohabitation. Three women reported that contact between father and child had been lost because the father simply could not be bothered to maintain contact. One of these women reported that she had given her former partner a choice: either he was to see his child more often, or not at all. He chose not at all. Two other women suggested that contact between father and child had been lost because her former partner refused to see *her*, abandoning his child in the process. In the last case, contact between father and child had been lost because the father no longer lived in Britain.

It seems unlikely that the experiences of these 6 women differ markedly from those of women whose *marriages* have ended. A great many divorced men lose touch with their children, and for reasons no better than those cited above. Cohabiting fatherhood can entail reduced parental commitment, but it does not do so necessarily. Indeed, the majority of unmarried absent fathers studied here gave their children not only their names and some financial support, but their physical presence as well.

What if they had married?

Finally, we asked women whose cohabitation had ended whether they thought that not being legally married might have contributed in any way to the breakdown of their relationship. This proved to be a question which elicited a remarkable degree of consensus among our respondents, with 23 out of 28 women reporting that no such effect had existed. Their relationships are likely to have ended for a variety of reasons (that we did not study) but not, it seems, because they had remained unmarried.

There were, however, 5 women who felt that remaining unmarried may have contributed to the breakdown of their relationship with their former partner. Four of these women reported that marriage would have made it more difficult for them to separate, thus giving the relationship more chances to survive; while one women suggested that marriage might have made her partner feel more secure, implying that his insecurity contributed to the ending of their relationship.

Our study barely scratches the surface of the implications and consequences of cohabitation breakdown for women and children, much less for fathers. It seems clear that any further study would be greatly enhanced by exploring in more depth the circumstances leading to cohabitation breakdown, as well as by the inclusion of cohabiting fathers in both intact and broken relationships.

Notes

1. Kiernan and Esthaugh, op.cit., 1993.
2. Jonathan Bradshaw and Jane Millar, *Lone Parent Families in the UK*, HMSO 1992, chapter 2.
3. Kiernan, op.cit., 1989, p.39.
4. Jo Roll, *Lone Parents in the European Community*, Family Policy Studies Centre, 1992.
5. Jane Millar, 'Lone Mothers' in C Glendinning and Jane Millar (eds), *Women and Poverty in Britain*, Wheatsheaf, 1987.
6. There was an 8 to 9 month gap between the birth of the 4 year old child and our original survey in 1988: enough time for relationships to change. Accordingly, all of the women who were identified as 'cohabiting mothers' in the original 1988 survey were asked in interviews in 1993 if their present (former) partner or husband was the other parent of their 4 year old child. All women who were continuing to cohabit and all women who had married after having children responded positively to this question. In fact, 2 women whose cohabitation had ended in breakdown indicated that the identity of the father was not known to them. In these 2 cases, we have assumed that the former partner was not the child's father.
7. One woman, whose partner had died, was excluded from these analyses, leaving a base of 28 formerly-cohabiting mothers.

8 The policy implications of long-term cohabitation

The critical question which informed our study of cohabiting mothers was why increasing numbers of women were remaining unmarried after having children. In assessing the policy implications of long-term cohabitation, we return to that question and add a further key issue: is it likely that most long-term cohabiting mothers ultimately will marry? It is evident that any call for changes in policy or law arising from long-term *parental* cohabitation would depend, in part at least, on the answers to both of these questions.

Of course, our study does not allow us to argue that precisely one percentage or another of long-term cohabiting couples with children ultimately will marry or not marry; although we would note that the longer women cohabit, the less likely they appear to marry. But we are able to speculate on the chances that long-term cohabitation will end in marriage, in the light of the reasons given by long-term cohabiting mothers for not marrying so far. And in doing so, we confront both of the key questions which inform our following discussion of the policy implications of long-term cohabitation.

Why haven't they married and will they?

Our study identified three key reasons why long-term cohabiting mothers had not married: the high cost of weddings, a fear of divorce, and the wish to avoid the institution of marriage itself. In addition, a range of other reasons were identified which could be summarised as factors which were delaying marriage. Remaining unmarried was a complex process, and often seemed to stem as much from having decided not to marry, as from having not decided to marry. Cohabiting mothers sometimes reported more than one reason for remaining unmarried; and, of course, the impact of some reasons was likely to be greater than that of other reasons.

For example, about 1 in 5 long-term cohabiting mothers reported that they had not married *yet*; that is, something was delaying marriage, such as a not-yet-finalised divorce, the desire to finish a course of education, falling pregnant again, being too busy at work and so on. Among all the long-term cohabiting mothers we interviewed in 1992, these women had lived with their partners for the shortest period and seemed the most likely to join the flow from cohabiting-motherhood into married-motherhood. Indeed, they probably have done so already.

Similarly, just over 1 in 4 long-term cohabiting mothers cited the high cost of weddings as a reason for not marrying. Although we have no way of knowing for sure, it seems improbable that a lack of money would permanently deter long-term cohabiting parents from marriage: either the attraction of a big white wedding will fade as they get older (there are other ways of marrying) or the added years will bring enough money to foot the bill. Either way, it seems likely that these women also will join the flow from cohabiting-motherhood into married-motherhood.

Much less certain is the fate of almost 1 in 3 long-term cohabiting mothers who cited a fear or dislike of divorce as their reason for not marrying. Indeed, in speculating on the chances of these women marrying, we come up against a considerable irony: the trauma involved in the process of divorcing – the effects of which may last for many years afterwards – seemingly deter some cohabiting mothers from marrying. If the divorce process was less confrontational, or divorce perhaps easier to obtain, then it seems likely that more long-term cohabiting mothers would marry.

Finally, we come to long-term cohabiting mothers who reported that they were deterred from marrying by the idea of marriage itself. Just over half of the long-term cohabiting mothers we interviewed expressed a wish to avoid marriage. In the strong version (reported by 1 in 5), this appeared to be based upon an ideologically-informed aversion to marriage. In the weaker version (expressed by 30 per cent), women simply could see no advantages in marriage. Neither group, in other words, could find reasons to marry: it seems reasonable to assume that for the foreseeable future at least, they will remain *cohabiting* mothers.

Our speculations so far suggest that as many as one-half of long-term cohabiting mothers, perhaps more, will not marry their partners, at least in the foreseeable future. However, our conjectural analysis of their chances of marrying has left out the one aspect of their lives that is, arguably, the most likely to encourage them to marry: their children. The principal reason for marrying given by the large majority of women who became mothers while cohabiting – whether or not they had married – was to ensure the security of their children. A substantial minority (1 in 4) of cohabiting women who married *before* having children also cited their children's security as a reason for marrying. Again, while we have no way of knowing for sure, it is possible that even women who object to the institution of marriage might be tipped into it by the wishes of their children, or by their desire to protect their children's interests.[1]

Aside from the fact that the foregoing discussion has ignored the possibility of cohabitation breakdown,[2] it may seem to have privileged legal marriage as an end that should be sought by all cohabiting women. Given disparities in earnings potential (and pension entitlement) between men and women, and legislation which tends to favour married couples (inheritance, maintenance, property), perhaps marriage is the best option, particularly for women with children. But to suggest this was not our aim. Rather, we wished to see if it was possible to gain an overall picture of the chances that long-term cohabiting mothers will marry ultimately and bring their own, and their children's, legal position into line that of with married parents. The implications for policy must be different if even long-term cohabitation tends to end in marriage.

Policy implications

Within what policy context should the implications of this research be placed? Britain does not have an explicit family policy, in the sense that specific courses of action are adopted by those in power in order to achieve specific goals. British political parties do not set their agenda in family terms. British governments of recent history at least have been notable more for their rhetoric, than for their formulation of policies that keep families in mind. Developments in family life are rarely publicly debated – and then usually in terms only of its demise, pending or apparent.

That is not to say that social policy affecting families has absent nor, indeed, neutral in relation to what constitutes a *proper* family.[3] Historically, and today, countless policy decisions impinge upon families, whether taken by politicians, in Whitehall or by local officials.[4] There are, as well, countless acts of legislation directed at shaping and regulating how men and women arrange their lives together. Through the Law – underpinned by other social institutions such as (most particularly) the Church and Monarchy – the force of these policies generally has been to recognise and protect one specific form of living arrangement: legal marriage. In 1753, Lord Hardwicke's Marriage Act privileged marriage above other relationships; for the next two centuries, that privilege was protected by law:

> So long as it remains public policy to support the institution of marriage, the law must necessarily distinguish between spouses and those who, whether by choice or force of circumstances, live together without getting married.[5]

Recent developments in Britain, however, (and in most other EC member states) point towards a shifting of emphasis away from the family as an social institution that needs buttressing, and towards families as

103

'person-supporting networks'.[6] That is, broader legal conceptions of marriage gradually are being admitted in order to widen the net of those who may be deemed financially responsible for each other. This is not in fact a wholly new development in Britain, but has been gaining force through the transformation of family law over the post-war period. In consequence, Parker argues that

> Family law has abandoned much of its punitive and negative character and presents an appearance of gender neutrality and non-interference. It is less concerned with legal status than with economic reality. Marriage is being displaced by 'family' and the wife is being displaced by the mother. Rather than being a primary moral and social regulator, modern family law has become one of a number of systems that demarcate the boundary between the family and the State and its particular function is to contain support obligations within the private sphere.[7]

One inevitable outcome of this transformation has been the gradual recognition of cohabitation, *in virtually every nook and cranny of law which has an impact on domestic relationships*,[8] and of the status of parent as opposed to that of married man or married woman. As Glendon writes

> Where there are children, but no marriage, certain duties of mutual support and maintaining children are imposed on parents. It makes no difference whether the couple is married or not. The law treats them as mother and father for the sake of the child.[9]

It is this history and transformation of public policy towards marriage which is perhaps the most appropriate context within which the implications of long-term cohabitation should be assessed. Accordingly, we end our report by addressing two questions: First, is long-term *parental* cohabitation a threat to legal marriage? Secondly, whatever its impact on legal marriage, can long-term cohabitation fulfil the economic role – as a person-supporting network – that is increasingly expected by government?

Is long-term cohabitation a threat to legal marriage?

Our study provides little evidence that long-term parental cohabitation threatens the institution of marriage. First, we have seen that among cohabiting mothers there is a steady flow from cohabiting-motherhood into married-motherhood, dependent for its timing on events related primarily to the private lives of the cohabitants and their families. Indeed, like 'nubile' cohabitation (a lifestyle taken up by childfree people in their twenties and early thirties as a prelude or an alternative to marriage) parental cohabitation is often a transitional stage, ending for many men and women when one or both is free to *re*marry. General Household Survey data indicate that fewer than 1 in 10 cohabiting women with children remain unmarried for more than 10 years.[10] Our speculations above suggest that fewer than 1 in 2 of these *long-term* cohabiting mothers will remain unmarried indefinitely.

Secondly, our study suggests that the family lives of long-term cohabiting couples do not differ substantially from the lives of married couples. If any differences could be discerned at all, it was that married women who do not live with their husbands before marriage tend to be *less* egalitarian in attitude and behaviour than women who do cohabit – whether or not the latter ultimately marry. Long-term cohabiting parents appeared as likely or unlikely to share household tasks, leisure and problems. They were as likely or unlikely to hold the same views on a range of social and family issues. Long-term cohabiting mothers were as happy or unhappy as other mothers. From our research, and that of others,[11] it seems likely that children have a greater impact on household organisation and marital harmony than the legal arrangements that bind, or do not bind, couples to one another.

Rather than constituting a threat to marriage, then, long-term cohabiting families more plausibly represent the revival of *social marriage*,[12] reflecting by their very existence, the modern-day diminishment of social norms which sanctioned only particular ways of living and condemned all others. As such, however, long-term cohabiting parents appear to have established lives which differ from those of married parents almost entirely in terms of the outside institutional world of schools, church and state. It seems likely that in the domestic sphere that there is more variation *within* long-term cohabiting and marital relationships than between them.[13]

Can long-term cohabitation provide the financial support network that is increasingly expected of marriage?

A small, highly-educated and seemingly affluent segment notwithstanding, the large majority of long-term cohabiting couples with children live in disadvantaged economic circumstances. Poorly educated, often unemployed, living in state housing and dependent upon state benefits, long-term cohabiting parents seem unlikely to be able to provide large measures of 'people support' insofar as this might require financial resources.

Furthermore, long-term cohabiting parents seem unlikely to have many assets to pass on to their children or surviving partners: state benefits cannot be bequeathed; occupational pensions are rarely a feature of low-level, low-paid employment. Our study suggests, moreover, that cohabiting parents with assets to bequeath – a house, a pension, some savings – tend to be the ones who marry soonest: the economic circumstances of cohabiting women who married *after* having children were better than those of still-cohabiting women; the best-off financially among women who were *continuing* to cohabit were those who reported that they had simply not yet got around to marrying. Most marriages may no longer be about preserving landed estates and titles, but marrying seemingly remains an economic transaction, practised most often by those with something to transact. [14]

In addition to having few financial resources or labour market advantages which would permit them to act as 'people-support networks', long-term cohabiting parents displayed a high degree of ignorance about the legal position of cohabiting fathers and their children; and seemed likely to be as unaware of their own legal position as unmarried partners. [15] Our focus on the legal relationship between cohabiting fathers and their children revealed that no cohabiting couples had taken steps to endow fathers with parental rights or responsibilities, although a tiny group had done so after cohabitation had broken down, while a few others had written wills naming the father as guardian in the event of the mother's death.

Most commonly, however, steps had not been taken to establish a legal relationship between father and child. This appeared largely to be the result of cohabiting parents' ignorance of the law, although two mothers reported that they had received relevant information through their children's schools. If the aim of policy is to encourage individual families to take fuller responsibility for family members, in order to contain – in Parker's words – *support obligations within the private sphere*, then it makes sense for information to be made more widely available to cohabiting parents about the consequences of not marrying. It is likely that this could be accomplished with relative ease. In France, for example, the Government Information Service publishes a guide to the legal situation of cohabitants, *Le Concubinage vos Droits.* [16] A similar booklet outlining the legal position of cohabitants, and of cohabiting parents and their children, could be made available to British cohabiting parents when they register their child's birth.

However, it is important to make the point that although the law can be used to enforce parental obligations (through the Child Support Agency, for example), recourse to the law is not always necessary. Our study suggests that cohabiting fathers readily take responsibility for their children, even after cohabitation breakdown. Only a small minority of formerly-cohabiting mothers reported that their now-absent partners did not keep in regular touch with their children: well over half reported that father and child saw each other at least once a week; about half received financial support for their children from their former partners. It seems self-evident that more information, more widely available, about the legal rights and obligations of cohabiting parents would be advantageous to cohabitants and policy-makers alike. But the evidence suggests, none the less, that the willingness of individual men and women to fashion lives together outside legal marriage encompasses the acceptance of obligations where they exist.

Should the state act to remove all legal distinctions between cohabitation and marriage? This question is a focus for debate in most Western European countries, including Sweden;[17] and can be given at least two, inherently oppositional, negative answers: No, because to do so would undermine legal marriage; No, because to do so would create a legal relationship where, arguably, none was sought or wanted. The 'yes vote' might argue, in company it would seem with some lawyers and law-makers,[18] that *not* to legislate is to perpetrate distinctions between families that are increasingly untenable in a modern, multi-cultural, essentially secular society.

Our study is able to contribute to this debate only obliquely, through its assessment of the likely impermanence of long-term cohabitation when children are involved. It seems probable that the need, and rationale, for legislative equality would change if even long-term cohabitation largely tended to end in marriage. And, indeed, we have noted that for many cohabitants with children, perhaps the majority, cohabitation is a transitional stage that ends in marriage. But what about long-term cohabiting mothers who will not marry? More importantly, what about their children?

We have suggested that long-term parental cohabitation is one reflection of the continuing attenuation of social norms which in the past have enforced sanctioned ways of living. That is, some part of the growth in modern-day cohabitation arises from the attempt made by men and women to create ways of living that make sense to them individually, whatever the dictates of tradition. Insofar as such men and women have children, the imposition by the state of equal rights and obligations as between married-parenthood and cohabiting-parenthood obviates this attempt, arguably with considerable justification. Cohabiting couples who wish to avoid rights and obligations may be advised also to avoid having children.

Notes

1. When questioned directly, fewer than 1 in 3 long-term cohabiting mothers said that they had no intention of marrying their partners. See Tables 5.3 and 5.4.
2. Unlike marriage, the beginnings and endings of cohabitation are, by its very nature, unrecorded events. Of the 166 'cohabiting women' from the 1988 survey who agreed to be interviewed, 32 were identified subsequently as having experienced cohabitation breakdown. We have no way of knowing whether this under- or over-estimates the rate of breakdown among cohabiting couples with children, or whether it reflects that rate accurately. Therefore we have chosen not to speculate on the chances that long-term cohabiting mothers will separate from their partners,

nor on the potential relationship between differing reasons for not marrying and the likelihood of cohabitation breakdown.

3. Perhaps the most obvious, and certainly the most pervasive, image of the proper family is that of the breadwinning father, dependent, home-making mother and their 2 children; which has underlined and continues to underline much social security, education and employment legislation. The literature examining the impact of public and social policy on families and family members is enormous; a landmark publication was Hilary Land, *Women and Economic Dependency*, Equal Opportunities Commission, 1986.

4. We are thinking here not just of policy decisions intended to affect families but also of the unintended consequences of decisions taken to meet other objectives.

5. *Bromley's Family Law, 1976*, quoted in Mansfield and Collard, op.cit., 1988, p.12.

6. See *Families and Policies: Evolutions and Trends, 1989-1990*, European Observatory on National Family Policies, EC, 1992.

7. Parker, op.cit., 1990, p.97.

8. Parker, ibid., p.148.

9. Mary Ann Glendon, 'The New Marriage and the New Property' in John Eekelaar and S. Katz, *Marriage and Cohabitation in Contemporary Societies*, Toronto, 1980.

10. Kiernan and Estaugh, op.cit., Chapter 2.

11. See in particular, Kiernan and Estaugh's 1993 re-analysis of British Social Attitudes data.

12. Parker, op.cit., 1990, p.4.

13. This point is made also by Kiernan and Estaugh, who question whether there are any real differences in the private domain between cohabiting and marital unions. Kiernan and Estaugh, op.cit., 1993, Chapter 10.

14. Unlike married couples who are automatically entitled to benefits from their partner's occupational pension schemes, surviving cohabitants are rarely entitled to pension benefits, and then only if they have been financially dependent upon the deceased. See Kiernan and Estaugh, ibid., 1993, Chapter 7.

15. See Chapter 6 note 3.

16. Centre National d'Information et de Documentation des Femmes et des Familles (CNIDFF), 1992, Le Concubinage vos Droits, Paris. Quoted in Kiernan and Estaugh, op.cit., 1993, Chapter 9.

17. For a summary of recent changes to family law in European Community Member States to take account of cohabitation, see European Observatory on National Family Policies, op.cit., 1992, Chapter VI. For a discussion of cohabitation law in Sweden, and continuing debates there, see Kiernan and Estaugh, ibid., 1993, Chapter 9.

18. According to Parker (op.cit., 1990, p.127) '... discourses and perceptions of justice have become partially detached from the rhetoric of marital rights and duties so that individual law-makers, either judges or parliamentarians, are at least nagged by doubts when a remedy available to a spouse is withheld from someone else who appears to be in the same situation'.

Appendix 1   The selection of cohabiting mothers

In the text, we note that the women interviewed for the current study were selected from among respondents to a postal survey conducted by PSI in 1988. The focus of that study was the operation of maternity rights legislation; the sample for it was drawn from Child Benefit records held by the DSS.

Table A1.1 summarises the legal marital status and living arrangements of respondents to the 1988 survey. This information was obtained by first asking women to indicate their legal marital status by ticking the appropriate box; and secondly, by asking them to indicate who else lived in their household: husband/partner, own children, husband/partner's children, and so on. From this information, we identified 347 women who said that they were single, separated, divorced or widowed *and* that they were living with a husband/partner. These women were designated 'cohabiting women' for the purposes of this study, and preliminary questionnaires sent to all for whom the DSS had names and addresses. The 'married women' to whom preliminary questionnaires were sent also were drawn from among respondents who reported that their legal marital status was married and that they were living with a husband/partner.

The 'cohabiting women' we identified in this way represented 7 per cent of the initial 1988 sample of new mothers. We do not wish to suggest, however, that 7 per cent of new mothers in 1988 were cohabiting. In her path-breaking survey of family formation, Dunnell (1979) suggested that the extent of cohabitation may be underestimated because women in such unions describe themselves as married and use their partner's name.[1] A re-analysis of General Household Survey data for 1986-89 by Haskey and Kelly (1991) suggested that inconsistencies in response were relatively rare between *de facto* marital status and legal marital status. It may be that the passage of a decade or so has increased the social acceptability of cohabitation to the extent that fewer cohabiting women feel obliged to describe their living arrangements as 'marriage'. Regardless, the important point to note is that our method of establishing respondents' marital status in the 1988 survey leaves open the possibility that there were more 'cohabiting mothers' than the 347 we identified.

Note

1.   Karen Dunnell, *Family Formation Survey*, London, HMSO, 1979.

Table A1.1 Marital status and living arrangements, all respondents to the 1988 Maternity Rights Survey

	Number of women	%
Living with husband/partner	4250	85
Legal marital status:		
married	3903	
single	269	
separated	10	
divorced	66	
widowed	2	
Lone mothers	741	15
Legal marital status:		
married	40	
single	476	
separated	136	
divorced	84	
widowed	5	
Base: all women	*4991*	*100*

Table A1.2 Characteristics of 'cohabiting mothers' according to participation in 1992 study

	Column percentages	
	In study	Not in study
Age in 1988		
16-20	17	19
21-24	27	33
25-29	30	25
30-34	18	18
35+	8	5
Marital status in 1988		
Single	76	82
Divorced	20	15
Separated	3	3
Widowed	1	1
Average number of children after 1988 birth	1.6	1.6
No more children intended	25	20
Highest qualification		
None	22	30
CSE below grade 1	10	19
O level/CSE	16	22
A level or higher	23	12
Vocational/other	28	28
Father's job		
Non-manual	31	17
Manual	52	52
Unemployed	15	25
Base:	*156*[*]	*189*

Note: The information shown in this table is derived from the 1988 Maternity Rights Survey.

[*]   10 'married women' were subsequently included as cohabiting women after interviews were carried out in 1992.

Table A1.3 Characteristics of 'married mothers' according to participation in 1992 study

		Column percentages
	In study	Not in study
Age in 1988		
16-20	11	12
21-24	18	22
25-29	18	22
30-34	43	38
35+	7	5
Average number of children after 1988 birth	2.0	1.9
No more children intended	37	38
Highest qualification		
None	29	32
CSE below grade 1	10	10
O level/CSE	11	13
A level or higher	29	25
Vocational/other	21	22
Father's job		
Non-manual	44	33
Manual	42	50
Unemployed	10	11
Base:	*172*[*]	*509*

Note: The information shown in this table is derived from the 1988 Maternity Rights Survey.

* 10 'married women' were subsequently included as cohabiting women after interviews were carried out in 1992.

Appendix 2 Additional tables

Table A2.1 Selected demographic and household characteristics of cohabiting mothers, according to previous marital history

	Number of women	
Average age	34	30
Average no. children	2.5	2.0
Has no qualifications	7	16
Current partner married previously	7	16
Stepchildren in household	1	3
Father's job W/C	11	18
Household income:		
£12,000 pa or less	11**	23*
Over £18,000 pa	2**	10*
Family credit received:		
In last 3 years	3	12
Currently	2	5
Income support received	5	17
Owner occupiers	13	33
Base: all continuing to cohabit mothers	*18*	*59*

*   8 'never married' cohabiting mothers did not provide information about household income.

**   3 'previously married' cohabiting mothers did not provide information about household income.

Table A2.2 Economic activity of cohabiting mothers, according to previous marital history

	Legally married before	Never legally married
Women in paid work	9	24
Current partner unemployed	5	12
- average duration of unemployment		
(months)	24.0	24.6
Both partners in work	8	23
Neither partner in work	4	14
Base: all continuing to cohabit mothers	*18*	*59*

Table A2.3 Reasons for not working

Column percentages

	Long-term cohabiting mothers	Cohabited pre-maritally		Non-cohab. married mothers	Cohabitation ended
		Married after baby	Married before baby		
Prefers not to work	27	(7)	32	33	(-)
Partner's preference	23	(2)	4	16	(-)
Mothers with small children should not work outside home	43	(5)	25	28	(6)
Cannot find paid job	9	(2)	4	2	(2)
Cannot find paid job with convenient hours/ in convenient location	43	(12)	39	44	(8)
Cannot earn enough to pay for childcare	36	(12)	32	30	(10)
Cannot find suitable childcare	16	(3)	25	14	(6)
Base: all women	*44*	*22*	*28*	*43*	*19*

Note: ( ) denotes actual number

Table A2.4 Reasons for being in paid employment

Column percentages

| | Long-term cohabiting mothers | Cohabited pre-maritally | | Non-cohab. married mothers | Cohabitation ended |
		Married after baby	Married before baby		
I enjoy working	82	66	83	69	(8)
Need money for basics	61	55	62	45	(11)
To earn money of my own	55	31	28	27	(5)
To follow my career	39	38	45	27	(2)
To earn money for extras	49	62	55	74	(8)
For company of others	70	62	86	63	(10)
Working is normal thing to do	24	7	21	8	(0)
Base: women in paid work N =	*33*	*29*	*29*	*49*	*13*

Note: ( ) denotes actual number

Appendix 3

The questionnaires

TIME INTERVIEW STARTED

(25 - 28)

WOMEN WITH CHILDREN
MAIN QUESTIONNAIRE

EMPLOYMENT AND LEISURE

First of all, I'd like to ask you some questions about work and leisure.

As you know, you were selected for today's interview because just over 4 years ago you took part in some research about women who had recently had a baby. That would have been a few months after .... (4 YEAR OLD CHILD'S NAME) was born.

Q.1   Were you working in a paid job during the time you were pregnant with ....
      (CHILD)?

	(29)
YES	1
NO	2
(DON'T KNOW)	9

CHECK CURRENT EMPLOYMENT STATUS FROM CONTACT SHEET

Q.2   In the questionnaire you sent us, you said you were .... (CURRENT
      EMPLOYMENT STATUS). Can I just check, is that still the case? CODE
      CURRENT SITUATION.

	(30)
WORKING	1 - ASK Q.3
NOT NOW WORKING	2 - GO TO Q.17

Q.3   Other than any period of maternity leave, have you worked continuously since
      .... (CHILD) was born? NB: MATERNITY LEAVE CAN BE UP TO SIX
      MONTHS AFTER A BIRTH.

	(31)
YES	1 - ASK Q.4
NO	2 - GO TO Q.7

Q.4   Have you worked in the same job throughout this period?

	(32)
YES	1 - ASK Q.5a
NO	2 - GO TO Q.7

IF YES AT Q.1 AND Q.4 ASK Q.5a (OTHERS GO TO Q.7)

Q.5a   Is that the same job you had been doing while you were pregnant with ....
       (CHILD)?

	(33)
YES, SAME JOB	1 - ASK Q.5b
NO, DIFFERENT JOB	2 - GO TO Q.6

Q.5b   Was it exactly the same job at the same level?

	(34)
YES, SAME JOB GRADE/LEVEL	1 ⎤ GO TO
JOB NOT GRADED	2 ⎦ Q.11
NO, ON DIFFERENT JOB/GRADE/LEVEL	3 - ASK Q.6
(DON'T KNOW)	9 - GO TO Q.11

IF DIFFERENT JOB AT Q.5a OR DIFFERENT JOB LEVEL ASK Q.6
Q.6   Why did you go to a different job/job level after .... (CHILD) was born?
PROBE FULLY

(35)	(36)
(37)	(38)
(39)	(40)
(41)	(42)

NOW GO TO Q.11

IF 'NO' AT Q.3 OR Q.4 ASK Q.7

Q.7 What was your <u>main job</u> during this time? PROMPT FOR FULL DETAILS
OF TITLE AND WORK DONE. RECORD <u>ONE</u> JOB ONLY.
(TAKE RESPONDENT'S DEFINITION OF MAIN JOB, WHETHER
DEFINED BY PAY, TIME OR SKILLS).

JOB TITLE: _____   (43-46)

WORK DONE: _____

_____

Q.8a When did you start working in that job?

WRITE IN MONTH [|]   (47,48)

<u>AND</u> YEAR 19 [|]   (49,50)

(DON'T KNOW)   9 (51)

Q.8b Are you still working in that job?

(52)
YES   1 - GO TO Q.9

NO   2 - ASK Q.8c

Q.8c When did you leave that job?

WRITE IN MONTH [|]   (53,54)

<u>AND</u> YEAR 19 [|]   (55,56)

(DON'T KNOW)   9 (57)

Q.9 Did you have any other jobs <u>at the same time</u> as that main job?

(58)
YES - MORE THAN ONE JOB   1
NO-ONE JOB ONLY   2
(DON'T KNOW)   9

Q.10a Did your <u>main job</u> after .... (CHILD) was born involve the same type of work
that you did before he/she was born?

(59)
YES   1 - GO TO Q.11

NO   2 - ASK Q.10b

NEVER WORKED BEFORE   3 ⎤ GO TO
(DON'T KNOW)   9 ⎦ Q.11

Q.10b Why did you change your type of work? PROBE FULLY

(60)	(61)
(62)	(63)
(64)	(65)
(66)	(67)

ASK ALL CURRENTLY IN WORK
CHECK CONTACT SHEET FOR JOB TITLE

Q.11   In the questionnaire you returned to us you said you were working as
        as .... JOB TITLE. Can I just check, are you still in that job?

                                                        (68)
                                          YES   1 - GO TO BOX AT
                                                      FOOT OF PAGE

                                          NO   2 - ASK Q.12

Q.12   What is the title of the job you do now? What do you do? PROMPT FOR
        TITLE AND DETAILS OF WORK DONE
                                                        (69-72)

        JOB TITLE: ....

        WORK DONE: ....

        ....

                                                        (73,74)
Q.13   How many hours a week do you usually work?

                        WRITE IN [   ] HOURS

                                  (DON'T KNOW)   9 (75)

Q.14   Are you an employee or self employed?
                                                        (76)
                                          EMPLOYEE   1
                                       SELF-EMPLOYED   2

Q.15   What business are your employers/are you in? What does the firm or
        organisation do or make, or what service do they provide?
        WRITE IN FULL DETAILS

                                                        (77-79)

                                                        (80) BLANK

┌───┐
│ ALL CURRENTLY IN WORK: GIVE SELF-COMPLETION TO RESPONDENT.   │
├───┤
│ I'd now like you to turn to page 1 of this booklet and   │
│ answer Q.16.   │
│   │
│ Q.16 We are interested in the reasons why you are   │
│   currently working in a paid job. Please tick all   │
│   those things which were important in influencing your │
│   decision to work at this time. Tick all items that   │
│   apply.   │
├───┤
│ NOW GO TO PAGE 6 AND Q.25a   │
└───┘

*

IF <u>NOT</u> CURRENTLY IN WORK (Q.2) ASK Q.17 (OTHERS TO GO TO Q.25)

Q.17   Have you worked at any time since .... (CHILD) was born?

		(11)
YES	1	- ASK Q.18a
NO	2	- GO TO BOX AT TOP OF PAGE 6

Q.18a What was your <u>main job</u> during this time? PROMPT FOR FULL DETAILS OF JOB TITLE AND WORK DONE. RECORD ONE JOB ONLY. (TAKE RESPONDENT'S DEFINITION OF MAIN JOB, WHETHER DEFINED BY PAY, TIME OR SKILLS)

JOB TITLE: _____   (12-15)

WORK DONE: _____

_____

Q.18b When did you start working in that job?

WRITE IN MONTH [   ]   (16,17)

<u>AND</u> YEAR 19 [   ]   (18,19)

(DON'T KNOW)   9 (20)

Q.18c And when did you stop working in that job?

WRITE IN MONTH [   ]   (21,22)

<u>AND</u> YEAR 19 [   ]   (23,24)

(DON'T KNOW)   9 (25)

Q.19   Was that job full or part-time?

	(26)
FULL-TIME	1
PART-TIME	2
(DON'T KNOW)	9

Q.20   And were you an employee or self-employed?

	(27)
EMPLOYEE	1
SELF-EMPLOYED	2
(DON'T KNOW)	9

Q.21   What business were your employers/were you involved in? (What did the firm/organisation do or make, or what service did they provide)?

(28-30)

Q.22   Did you have any other jobs <u>at the same time</u> as that main job?

	(31)
YES - MORE THAN ONE JOB	1
NO-ONE JOB ONLY	2
(DON'T KNOW)	9

*

IF NOT CURRENTLY WORKING ('NO' AT Q.2) GIVE RESPONDENT
SELF-COMPLETION.

Please turn to page 2 of the self-completion booklet and
Q.23.

Q.23 We are interested in the reasons why you are not
      currently working in a job. Please tick those
      things which were important in influencing your
      decision not to work at this time. Please tick all
      that apply.

NOW ASK THIS GROUP OF RESPONDENTS Q.24

Q.24 When do you think you might start looking for paid work? PROMPT WITH
      PRECODES IF NECESSARY. CODE ONE ANSWER ONLY.

	(32)
QUITE SOON	1
IN A YEAR OR TWO	2
WHEN YOUNGEST CHILD IS AT PRIMARY SCHOOL	3
WHEN YOUNGEST CHILD IS AT SECONDARY SCHOOL	4
WHEN YOUNGEST CHILD LEAVES SCHOOL OR LEAVES HOME	5
OTHER - CODE AND WRITE IN	6
HAVE A JOB ALREADY ARRANGED	7
WOULD PREFER NOT TO WORK	8
(DON'T KNOW)	9

(33)	(34)
(35)	(36)

ASK ALL

Q.25a Have difficulties with childcare arrangements ever affected your ability to
       work?

	(37)
YES	1 - ASK Q.25b
NO	2 ⌉ GO TO
(DON'T KNOW)	9 ⌋ Q.26a

Q.25b In what way? PROBE FULLY

(38)	(39)
(40)	(41)
(42)	(43)
(44)	(45)

Q.26a <u>SHOW CARD 1</u>: I'm going to read out a list of activities and for each I'd like you to choose from this card the answer which best describes how often you have done that activity in the <u>last month</u>. READ OUT EACH OF 1-19 IN TURN AND CODE IN GRID.

ASK Q.26b FOR <u>EACH</u> ACTIVITY UNDERTAKEN AT Q.26a (IF NONE, GO TO Q.27)

Q.26b <u>SHOW CARD 2</u>: Who were you with when you last ... ACTIVITY? CODE ALL MENTIONED

	Q.26a: FREQUENCY					Q.26b: DID WITH ...								
	ONCE A WEEK OR MORE	ONCE A FORT-NIGHT	ONCE A MONTH	NOT AT ALL	(DK)	ALONE	CHILD-REN OWN HOUSE-HOLD	HUSBAND PARTNER	OTHER ADULTS FROM HOUSE-HOLD (NOT) PARTNER	PEOPLE FROM WORK	NEIGH-BOURS	FRIENDS	RELA-TIVES	(DK)
1. Go to library	1	2	3	4	9 (46)	1 (65)	1 (14)	1 (33)	1 (52)	1 (71)	1 (20)	1 (39)	1 (58)	9 (77)
2. Go swimming	1	2	3	4	9 (47)	1 (66)	1 (15)	1 (34)	1 (53)	1 (72)	1 (21)	1 (40)	1 (59)	9 (78)
3. Play a sport	1	2	3	4	9 (48)	1 (67)	1 (16)	1 (35)	1 (54)	1 (73)	1 (22)	1 (41)	1 (60)	9 (79)
4. Watch live sport	1	2	3	4	9 (49)	1 (68)	1 (17)	1 (36)	1 (55)	1 (74)	1 (23)	1 (42)	1 (61)	9 (80)
5. Go to a theatre or concert	1	2	3	4	9 (50)	1 (69)	1 (18)	1 (37)	1 (56)	1 (75)	1 (24)	1 (43)	1 (62)	9 (11)
6. Go to cinema	1	2	3	4	9 (51)	1 (70)	1 (19)	1 (38)	1 (57)	1 (76)	1 (25)	1 (44)	1 (63)	9 (12)
7. Go to a pub or club	1	2	3	4	9 (52)	1 (71)	1 (20)	1 (39)	1 (58)	1 (77)	1 (26)	1 (45)	1 (64)	9 (13)
8. Attend a religous service to take part in an act of worship (<u>not</u> to attend a wedding, funeral etc.)	1	2	3	4	9 (53)	1 (72)	1 (21)	1 (40)	1 (59)	1 (78)	1 (27)	1 (46)	1 (65)	9 (14)
9. Pay a social visit to someone's house	1	2	3	4	9 (54)	1 (73)	1 (22)	1 (41)	1 (60)	1 (79)	1 (28)	1 (47)	1 (66)	9 (15)
10. Go out for a meal	1	2	3	4	9 (55)	1 (74)	1 (23)	1 (42)	1 (61)	1 (80)	1 (29)	1 (48)	1 (67)	9 (16)
11. Work in the garden	1	2	3	4	9 (56)	1 (75)	1 (24)	1 (43)	1 (62)	1 (11)	1 (30)	1 (49)	1 (68)	9 (17)
12. Watch TV	1	2	3	4	9 (57)	1 (76)	1 (25)	1 (44)	1 (63)	1 (12)	1 (31)	1 (50)	1 (69)	9 (18)
13. Read a book or magazine	1	2	3	4	9 (58)	1 (77)	1 (26)	1 (45)	1 (64)	1 (13)	1 (32)	1 (51)	1 (70)	9 (19)
14. Go walking	1	2	3	4	9 (59)	1 (78)	1 (27)	1 (46)	1 (65)	1 (14)	1 (33)	1 (52)	1 (71)	9 (20)
15. Attend leisure activity groups (eg yoga, art, dance etc)	1	2	3	4	9 (60)	1 (79)	1 (28)	1 (47)	1 (66)	1 (15)	1 (34)	1 (53)	1 (72)	9 (21)
16. Attend evening classes to study	1	2	3	4	9 (61)	1 (80)	1 (29)	1 (48)	1 (67)	1 (16)	1 (35)	1 (54)	1 (73)	9 (22)
17. Attend meetings for local groups, politica/parties	1	2	3	4	9 (62)	1 (11)	1 (30)	1 (49)	1 (68)	1 (17)	1 (36)	1 (55)	1 (74)	9 (23)
18. Do unpaid voluntary work	1	2	3	4	9 (63)	1 (12)	1 (31)	1 (50)	1 (69)	1 (18)	1 (37)	1 (56)	1 (75)	9 (24)
19. Do other unpaid help for people outside your household	1	2	3	4	9 (64)	1 (13)	1 (32)	1 (51)	1 (70)	1 (19)	1 (38)	1 (57)	1 (76)	9 (25)
						CARD 03				CARD 04				CARD 05

MARITAL STATUS

ASK ALL:
I'd now like to ask you some questions about your marital status and living
arrangements.

Q.27 Thinking back to September/October 1988 when the earlier research was
carried out, were you and your partner at that time legally married, or were
you living together as a couple?

	(26)
MARRIED	1 - ASK Q.28
LIVING TOGETHER	2 - GO TO Q.48 (P.14)
NO PARTNER	3 - GO TO ANNEX Q'NAIRE

Q.28 When did you get married?

WRITE IN MONTH ☐☐ (27,28)

AND YEAR 19 ☐☐ (29,30)

(DON'T KNOW) 9 (31)

Q.29 And today, are you and your husband still marrried?

	(32)
YES	1 - ASK Q.30
NO	2 - GO TO Q.41 (P.12)

Q.30a Have you been married just once or more than once?

	(33)
ONCE	1
MORE THAN ONCE	2

Q.30b Has your husband been married just once, or more than once?

	(34)
ONCE	1
MORE THAN ONCE	2
(DON'T KNOW)	9

Q.31 Do you both use the same last name?

	(35)
YES	1
NO	2

Q.32a Did you and your husband live together for any length of time before getting
married?

	(36)
YES	1 - ASK Q.32b
NO	2 - GO TO BOX AT Q.38 (P.11)

Q.32b For about how long did you live together before getting married?

(37-39)

WRITE IN MONTHS ☐☐☐

DON'T KNOW/CAN'T REMEMBER 9 (40)

Please turn to page 3 of the self-completion booklet and
answer Q.33

Q.33 We are interested in why you and your husband first
      set up home together when you did. Please tick
      those things which were important in influencing the
      the point in your life when you first set up home
      together. <u>Please tick all that apply</u>

Q.34 We'd also like to know why you chose to live together as a couple, rather
      than get married straight away. What things would you say were important in
      influencing your decision to delay getting married? PROBE FULLY.

(41)	(42)
(43)	(44)
(45)	(46)
(47)	(48)

Q.35a Do you think there are any advantages in living together as a couple, rather
       than being married?

	(49)	
YES	1 -	ASK Q.35b
NO	2 ⌐	GO TO
(DON'T KNOW	9 ⌐	Q.36a

Q.35b What do you think the advantages are (of living together)? PROBE FULLY.

(50)	(51)
(52)	(53)
(54)	(55)
(56)	(57)

IF 'YES' AT Q.32a

Q.36a And do you think there are any disadvantages in living together compared with being married?

	(58)	
YES	1	- ASK Q.36b
NO	2 ⌉	GO TO BOX
(DON'T KNOW)	9 ⌋	AT Q.37

Q.36b What do you think the disadvantages are? (Of living together) PROBE FULLY

(59)	(60)
(61)	(62)
(63)	(64)
(65)	(66)

IF YES AT Q.32a:

Now turn to page 4 and and answer Q.37.

Q.37 We are also interested in why you and your husband chose to get married. Please tick those things which were important in influencing your decision to get married. <u>Tick all that apply.</u>

NOW GO TO PAGE 20 AND Q.74

IF NO AT Q.32a:

Please turn to page 5 and answer Q.38 of the self-completion booklet.

Q.38 We are interested in why you and your husband decided to get married. Please tick those things which were important in influencing your decision to get married. <u>Please tick all that apply.</u>

NOW ASK THIS GROUP OF RESPONDENTS Q.39a

Q.39a Do you think there are any advantages in being married, compared with living together as a couple?

	(67)	
YES	1	- ASK Q.39b
NO	2	] GO TO
(DON'T KNOW)	9	Q.40a

Q.39b What do you think the advantages are? (Of being married) PROBE FULLY

(68)	(69)
(70)	(71)
(72)	(73)
(74)	(75)

<u>IF NO AT Q.32a ASK Q.40a</u>
Q.40a And do you think there are any disadvantages in being married, compared with living together as a couple?

	(76)	
YES	1	- ASK Q.40b
NO	2	] GO TO
(DON'T KNOW)	9	Q.74 (P.20)

(77-80) BLANK

CARD 06

Q.40b What do you think those disadvantages are? (Of being married) PROBE FULLY

(11)	(12)
(13)	(14)
(15)	(16)
(17)	(18)

NOW GO TO PAGE 20 AND Q.74

IF NO AT Q.29 ASK Q.41
Q.41 Did you and your former husband live together for any length of time
      before you got married?

                                                              (19)
                                              YES   1 - ASK Q.42

                                               NO   2 ┐ GO TO
                                        (DON'T KNOW)   9 ┘ Q.43

Q.42 For about how long did you live together before getting married?

          WRITE IN [|] MONTHS   (20-22)

                                        (DON'T KNOW)   9   (23)

IF 'NO' AT Q.29 ASK Q.43
Q.43 And for how long were you married?

          WRITE IN MONTHS [|]   (24,25)

          AND YEARS   [|]   (26,27)

                                        (DON'T KNOW)   9   (28)

Q.44 What is your marital status now? Are you ... READ OUT

                                                              (29)
                                        divorced   1 ┐ ASK
                                       separated   2 ├ Q.45
                                        widowed   3 ┘
      ----
                   legally married to someone else   4 - GO TO Q.46

Q.45   Are you living with anyone now - as a couple I mean?

                                                            (30)
                                                   YES   1 - ASK Q.46a
                              ----
                                                   NO   2 - GO TO Q.74 (P.20)

IF REMARRIED OR LIVING WITH SOMEONE ASK Q.46a

Q.46a When did you get married/start living together?

         WRITE IN MONTH   ☐☐   (31,32)

         AND YEAR   19   ☐☐   (33,34)

                                   (DON'T KNOW)   9   (35)

Q.46b Had your partner/husband ever been married before?

                                                    (36)
                                          YES   1
                                          NO   2
                                  (DON'T KNOW)   9

Q.47   Do you both use the same last name?

                                                    (37)
                                          YES   1
                                          NO   2

            ┌─────────────────────────────────────┐
            │   NOW GO TO PAGE 20 AND Q.74   │
            └─────────────────────────────────────┘

IF 'LIVING TOGETHER' (CODE 2) AT Q.27 ASK Q.48
Q.48 Were you at that time ... READ OUT

	(38)
single (ie never married)	1
divorced	2
separated	3
widowed	4

Q.49 And today are you and your partner still living together, or have you married or separated?

	(39)
YES, STILL LIVING TOGETHER	1 - ASK Q.50a
MARRIED NOW	2 - GO TO Q.58 (P.17)
NO LONGER LIVING WITH PARTNER	3 - GO TO Q.68 (P.19)

Q.50a When did you and ... (PARTNER) start living together as a couple?
(NB: WHEN NEITHER PARTNER MAINTAINED A SEPARATE RESIDENCE)

WRITE IN MONTH ☐☐ (40,41)

AND YEAR 19 ☐☐ (42,43)

(DON'T KNOW) 9 (44)

Q.50b Had your partner ever been married before?

	(45)
YES	1
NO	2
(DON'T KNOW)	9

Q.51b Do you both use the same last name?

	(46)
YES	1
NO	2

Now please turn to page 6 of the self-completion booklet and answer Q.52.

Q.52 We are interested in why you and your partner set up home together when you did. Please tick those things which were important in influencing the point in your life when you first set up home together. Please tick all that apply.

✳

Q.53 We are also interested in why you and your partner have chosen not to
      get married. What things would you say were important in influencing
      your decision not to get married?
      PROBE FULLY

(47)	(48)
(49)	(50)
(51)	(52)
(53)	(54)

Q.54a Do you think there are any advantages in living together as a couple,
       compared with being married?

```
                                    (55)
                          YES        1  - ASK Q.54b
      ------------------------------------------------
                           NO        2 ] GO TO
                  (DON'T KNOW)        9 ] Q.55a
```

Q.54b What do you think the advantages are? (Of living together)
       PROBE FULLY

(56)	(57)
(58)	(59)
(60)	(61)
(62)	(63)

IF 'STILL LIVING TOGETHER' AT Q.49 ASK Q.55a
Q.55a And do you think there are any disadvantages in living together,
       compared with being married?

```
                                        (64)
                              YES        1  - ASK Q.55b
         -------------------------------------------------------------
                              NO         2  ] GO TO
                       (DON'T KNOW)      9  ] Q.56
```

Q.55b What do you think the disadvantages are? (Of living together)
       PROBE FULLY

(65)	(66)
(67)	(68)
(69)	(70)
(71)	(72)

Q.56   Do you think that you might someday get married to your partner?

```
                                        (73)
                              YES        1  ] GO TO BOX
                 UNCERTAIN/PERHAPS       2  ] AT Q.57
         -------------------------------------------------------------
                              NO         3  ] GO TO
                       (DON'T KNOW)      9  ] Q.74 (P.20)
```

Now please turn to page 7 of the self-completion
booklet and answer Q.57

Q.57 What things might be important in influencing your
     decision to get married someday? Please tick those
     things that might be important in influencing your
     decision. Tick all that apply.

NOW GO TO PAGE 20 AND Q.74

<u>IF MARRIED NOW AT Q.49 ASK Q.58a</u>

Q.58a When did you get married?

WRITE IN MONTH [|]   (74,75)

AND YEAR   19 [|]   (76,77)

(DON'T KNOW)   9   (78)

Q.58b Had your husband ever been married before?

                        (79)
                YES   1
                 NO   2
      (DON'T KNOW)   9

                   (80) BLANK

                   CARD 07

Q.59   For about how long did you live together before you got married?

WRITE IN [| |] MONTHS   (11-13)

(DON'T KNOW)   9   (14)

Q.60b Do you both use the same last name?

                        (15)
                 YES   1
                 NO   2

> Please turn to page 8 of the self-completion and answer Q.61
>
> Q.61 We are interested in why you and your partner first set up home together when you did. Please tick all those things which were important in influencing the point in your life when you first set up home together. <u>Tick all that apply.</u>

         ✱

Q.62   We would also like to know why you chose to live together as a couple, rather than get married straight away. What things would you say were important in influencing your decision to delay getting married? PROBE FULLY

(16)	(17)
(18)	(19)
(20)	(21)
(22)	(23)

Q.63 Do you think there are any advantages in living together as a couple compared with being married?

	(24)	
YES	1	- ASK Q.64
NO	2	GO TO Q.65a
(DON'T KNOW)	9	

Q.64 What do you think the advantages are? (Of living together) PROBE FULLY

(25)	(26)
(27)	(28)
(29)	(30)
(31)	(32)

Q.65a And do you think there are any disadvantages in living together, compared with being married?

	(33)	
YES	1	- ASK Q.65b
NO	2	GO TO Q.66
(DON'T KNOW)	9	

Q.65b What do you think the disadvantages are? (Of living together) PROBE FULLY

(34)	(35)
(36)	(37)
(38)	(39)
(40)	(41)

> Now turn to Q.66 on page 9 of the self-completion.
>
> Q.66 We are interested in why you and your husband decided to get married. Please tick all those things which were important in influencing your decision to get married. <u>Please tick all that apply.</u>

✱

Q.67a Do you think that getting married changed your relationship with your partner in any way?

	(42)		
YES	1	]	ASK
UNCERTAIN/PERHAPS	2		Q.67b
NO	3	]	GO TO
(DON'T KNOW)	9		Q.74

Q.67b In what way? PROBE FULLY

(43)	(44)
(45)	(46)
(47)	(48)
(49)	(50)

> NOW GO TO PAGE 20 AND Q.74

<u>IF NO LONGER LIVING WITH PARTNER AT Q.49 ASK Q.68</u>

Q.68 When was it that you and your partner first started living together?

WRITE IN MONTH [ ]   (51,52)

AND YEAR   19 [ ]   (53,54)

(DON'T KNOW)   9   (55)

Q.69 And when did you separate?

WRITE IN MONTH [ ]   (56,57)

AND YEAR   19 [ ]   (58,59)

(DON'T KNOW)   9   (60)

Q.70 Are you living with anyone now, as a couple I mean?

	(61)	
YES	1	- ASK Q.71
NO	2	] GO TO
(DON'T KNOW)	9	] Q.74

Q.71   Are you and your partner legally married, or are you living together as a couple?

	(62)
MARRIED	1
LIVING TOGETHER	2

Q.72   When did you get married/start living together?

WRITE IN MONTH   ☐☐   (63,64)

AND YEAR   19 ☐☐   (65,66)

(DON'T KNOW)   9   (67)

Q.73b   Do you both use the same last name?

	(68)
YES	1
NO	2

FOR ALL RESPONDENTS

Q.74   INTERVIEWER: CODE MARITAL STATUS - ONE CODE ONLY

		(69)
LIVES WITH ORIGINAL PARTNER AND:	ALWAYS MARRIED	1
	ALWAYS COHABITING	2
	FORMERLY COHABITING, NOW MARRIED	3
HAS NEW PARTNER AND:	FORMERLY MARRIED	4
	FORMERLY COHABITING	5
HAS NO PARTNER AND:	FORMERLY MARRIED	6
	FORMERLY COHABITING	7

NB: THE RELEVANT COMPARISON FOR CODING THIS QUESTION IS BETWEEN THE RESPONDENT'S STATUS IN <u>SEPTEMBER/OCTOBER 1988</u> (GIVEN AT Q.27) AND HER <u>CURRENT</u> STATUS

CHILDREN

CHECK CONTACT SHEET: TOTAL NUMBER OF CHILDREN [ ][ ]   (70,71)

AGE OF YOUNGEST CHILD [ ]   (72)

Q.75 Can I just check from the questionnaire you sent us a few weeks ago, you have ... child(ren) and the youngest is aged .... Is that correct? AMEND DETAILS AS NECESSARY

ONE CHILD ONLY	(73) 1 -	GO TO BOX AT Q.78
MORE THAN ONE CHILD	2 -	ASK Q.76

Q.76 Are any of your children step-children? That is: are they your (former) partner's children, or your own children from an earlier relationship?

YES	(74) 1 -	ASK Q.77a
NO	2]	GO TO BOX
(DON'T KNOW)	9]	AT Q.78

(75-80) BLANK

CARD 08

Q.77a Which ones are step-children? WRITE NAMES AND AGES IN GRID. ASK Q.77b FOR EACH STEP-CHILD

Q.77b And is ... (CHILD) from an earlier relationship of yours or of your partner's?

Q.77a NAME	AGE		Q.77b RESPONDENT'S	PARTNER'S	
	(11)	(12)	1	2	(23)
	(13)	(14)	1	2	(24)
	(15)	(16)	1	2	(25)
	(17)	(18)	1	2	(26)
	(19)	(20)	1	2	(27)
	(21)	(22)	1	2	(28)

ASK ALL

Please turn to Q.78 on page 10 of the self completion questionnaire.

Q.78 Please tick all those things which were important in influencing the point in your life when you had your first child. Please tick all that apply.   *

Now turn over to Q.79

Q.79 We'd like to ask you if you are hoping to have any children in the future. Please tick the appropriate box and follow the instructions given to answer either Q.80 or Q.81   *

CHECK THAT RESPONDENT FOLLOWS ROUTING. DO NOT READ OUT Q.80 OR Q.81 UNLESS ASKED TO.

IF 'A' AT Q.79 → Q.80 PLEASE TICK ANY OF THE FOLLOWING REASONS WHY YOU EXPECT TO HAVE MORE CHILDREN IN THE FUTURE. TICK ALL THAT APPLY   *

IF 'B' AT Q.79 → Q.81 PLEASE TICK ANY OF THE FOLLOWING REASONS WHY YOU ORIGINALLY CAME TO THE VIEW THAT YOU WOULD NOT HAVE ANY MORE CHILDREN. TICK ALL THAT APPLY   *

HOUSEHOLD COMPOSITION AND ORGANISATION

ASK ALL

Q.82 Does anyone else usually live here as part of your household, <u>in addition to</u> you and your partner/husband and children?

		(29)	
	YES	1	- ASK Q.83
	NO	2]	GO TO
	(DON'T KNOW)	9]	Q.86

Q.83 I'd like to get some details about the others in your household, starting with their names. WRITE IN NAMES OF ALL OTHERS IN HOUSEHOLD.

ASK Q.84 AND Q.85 FOR EACH OTHER PERSON

Q.84 <u>SHOW CARD 3</u>: What is the relationship of ... to you? WRITE IN TWO DIGIT CODE.

Q.85 <u>SHOW CARD 4</u>: Which one of the options on this card best describes the situation of ... in the last 7 days? WRITE IN TWO DIGIT CODE.

PERSON NO.	NAME	RELATIONSHIP (CARD 3)		ACTIVITY (CARD 4)	
1		(30)	(31)	(50)	(51)
2		(32)	(33)	(52)	(53)
3		(34)	(35)	(54)	(55)
4		(36)	(37)	(56)	(57)
5		(38)	(39)	(58)	(59)
6		(40)	(41)	(60)	(61)
7		(42)	(43)	(62)	(63)
8		(44)	(45)	(64)	(65)
9		(46)	(47)	(66)	(67)
10		(48)	(49)	(68)	(69)

```
CARD 3:  RELATIONSHIP

01 MOTHER
02 FATHER
03 GRANDMOTHER
04 GRANDFATHER
05 BROTHER
06 SISTER
07 OTHER RELATIVE
08 LODGER/BOARDER
09 OTHER NON RELATIVE
88 REFUSED
```

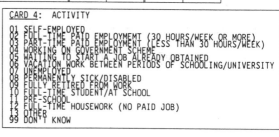

```
CARD 4:  ACTIVITY

01 SELF-EMPLOYED
02 FULL-TIME PAID EMPLOYMEMT (30 HOURS/WEEK OR MORE)
03 PART-TIME PAID EMPLOYMENT (LESS THAN 30 HOURS/WEEK)
04 WORKING ON GOVERNMENT SCHEME
05 WAITING TO START A JOB ALREADY OBTAINED
06 VACATION WORK BETWEEN PERIODS OF SCHOOLING/UNIVERSITY
07 UNEMPLOYED
08 PERMANENTLY SICK/DISABLED
09 FULLY RETIRED FROM WORK
10 FULL-TIME STUDENT/AT SCHOOL
11 PRE-SCHOOL
12 FULL-TIME HOUSEWORK (NO PAID JOB)
13 OTHER
99 DON'T KNOW
```

Q.86 How long have you lived in your present home?

	(70)	
LESS THAN ONE YEAR	1	- ASK Q.87
BETWEEN ONE AND THREE YEARS	2	GO TO
MORE THAN THREE YEARS	3	Q.88
(DON'T KNOW)	9	

Q.87 Did you own your previous home, or were you a tenant? PROMPT
WITH PRECODES IF NECESSARY

	(71)
OWNED/BUYING ON MORTGAGE	1
SHARED OWNERSHIP (PART OWNED/PART RENTED)	2
RENTED FROM COUNCIL, LA OR HOUSING ASSOCIATION	3
RENTED PRIVATELY	4
RENTED FROM EMPLOYER OR FREE WITH JOB	5
OTHER TENANCY	6
NON-HOUSEHOLDER IN PREVIOUS HOME (EG LIVED WITH PARENTS)	7
(DON'T KNOW)	9

ASK ALL
Q.88 Do you own your present home or are you a tenant? PROMPT
WITH PRECODES IF NECESSARY

	(72)
OWNED/BUYING ON MORTGAGE	1
SHARED OWNERSHIP (PART OWNED/PART RENTED)	2
RENTED FROM COUNCIL, LA OR HOUSING ASSOCIATION	3
RENTED PRIVATELY	4
RENTED FROM EMPLOYER OR FREE WITH JOB	5
OTHER TENANCY	6
NON-HOUSEHOLDER (EG LIVES WITH PARENTS)	7
(DON'T KNOW)	9

Q.89 **CHECK MARITAL STATUS AT Q.74**

	(73)	
CODES 1-5 - CURRENTLY MARRIED/COHABITING	1	- GO TO BOX AT Q.90
CODES 6,7 - NO PARTNER	2	- GO TO Q.105a (P.28)

Now turn to page 14 of the self-completion and answer
Q.90

Q.90 We are interested in who usually does the household
tasks in your household. Please tick the box below
which describes how the following tasks are divided up
or shared between you and your partner. <u>Tick one box
for each item.</u>

*

Now turn over, and answer Q.91

Q.91 Does anyone else inside or outside your household
usually help with these tasks? <u>Please tick all that
apply.</u>

*

Q.92   Thinking about your four year old now, who usually puts him/her to
bed at night, you or your partner?

		(74)
	RESPONDENT	1
	PARTNER	2
	BOTH EQUALLY	3
	SOMEONE ELSE	4
	(DON'T KNOW)	9

Q.93a Still thinking about your four year old, does your partner ever read
stories to him/her?

	(75)
YES	1 - ASK Q.93b

NO	2 ⌉ GO TO
(DON'T KNOW)	9 ⌋ Q.94a

Q.93b About how often does he read to him/her? Would it be ... READ
OUT

	(76)
EVERY DAY/NIGHT	1
3 OR 4 TIMES A WEEK	2
ONCE OR TWICE A WEEK	3
JUST ONCE IN A WHILE	4
OTHER - CODE & WRITE IN	5

(DON'T KNOW)	9

(77)

Q.94a Is there any activity that your four year old and your partner often do
together, just the two of them or just with other children?

	(78)
YES	1 - ASK Q.94b

NO	2 ⌉ GO TO BOX
(DON'T KNOW)	9 ⌋ AT Q.95a

(79,80) BLANK

CARD 09

Q.94b What activity is that? WRITE IN

(11)	(12)
(13)	(14)
(15)	(16)
(17)	(18)

Now turn to page 16 of the self-completion and answer
Q.95a and b.

Q.95a Thinking about your situation now, please tick the box
      which best describes who in your household has <u>ultimate</u>
      responsibility for each of the following. Tick <u>one</u> box
      for <u>each</u> of 1-4.   *

Q.95b And please tick the box which best describes who you
      think <u>should</u> have <u>ultimate</u> responsibility for each of
      the following. Tick <u>one</u> box for <u>each</u> of 1-4.   *

Q.96   <u>SHOW CARD 5</u>: People organise their household finances in
        different ways. Which <u>one</u> of the methods on this card comes closest
        to the way that you organise yours. It doesn't need to fit exactly -
        you should choose the nearest one. CODE ONE ANSWER ONLY

                                                                      (19)

                1. I LOOK AFTER ALL HOUSEHOLD MONEY EXCEPT
                        MY PARTNER'S PERSONAL SPENDING MONEY   1

                2. MY PARTNER LOOKS AFTER ALL THE HOUSEHOLD MONEY
                        EXCEPT MY PERSONAL SPENDING MONEY   2

            3. I AM GIVEN A HOUSEKEEPING ALLOWANCE, MY PARTNER LOOKS
                            AFTER THE REST OF THE MONEY   3

            4. MY PARTNER IS GIVEN A HOUSEKEEPING ALLOWANCE. I LOOK
                            AFTER THE REST OF THE MONEY   4

                5. WE SHARE AND MANAGE OUR HOUSEHOLD AND PERSONAL
                                    FINANCES JOINTLY   5

        6. WE SHARE AND MANAGE HOUSEHOLD FINANCES JOINTLY, BUT KEEP
                    OUR PERSONAL FINANCES COMPLETELY SEPARATE   6

                7. WE KEEP ALL OUR FINANCES COMPLETELY SEPARATE   7

    8. OTHER - CODE AND WRITE IN _ _ _ _ _ _ _ _ _ _ _ _ _ _ _   8

    _

    _

                                    (DON'T KNOW)   9

                                                        (20,21)

Q.97   So who has the <u>final</u> say in big financial decision?

	(22)
YOURSELF	1
YOUR PARTNER	2
BOTH EQUALLY	3
NEITHER	4
(DON'T KNOW)	9

Q.98a   Have you had a family holiday in the last 12 months?

	(23)	
YES	1	- ASK Q.98b

NO	2	GO TO
(DON'T KNOW)	9	Q.99a

Q.98b   How much did your last main family holiday cost, including spending money?

WRITE IN AMOUNT £ ☐☐☐☐   (24-27)

(DON'T KNOW)   9   (28)

Q.99a   As an individual - apart from your husband/partner that is - do you save regularly?

	(29)
YES	1
NO	2
(DON'T KNOW)	9

Q.99b   Do you have any insurance policies to protect you and your child(ren) in case your partner/husband should die or become disabled?

	(30)
YES	1
NO	2
(DON'T KNOW)	9

Q.100   In the last year, have you ever had to fall behind in your payment of ... READ OUT EACH IN TURN AND CODE IN GRID.

	YES	NO	NOT APPLIC.	(DON'T KNOW)	
1. Your mortgage or rent	1	2	0	9	(31)
2. Your gas bills	1	2	0	9	(32)
3. Your electricity bills	1	2	0	9	(33)
4. Hire purchase payments	1	2	0	9	(34)

Q.101a   Do you use paid childcare on a regular basis?

	(35)	
YES	1	- ASK Q.101b

NO	2	GO TO
(DON'T KNOW)	9	Q.102

Q.101b   How do you pay for childcare? Does the money come from ... CODE ONE ANSWER ONLY

	(36)
your personal funds or pay cheque	1
your partner's pay cheque	2
your joint money	3
or some other source - WRITE IN	4

(DON'T KNOW)   9   (37)

Q.102   And what about other expenses for your dependent child(ren)? For
        example, who pays for ... READ OUT AND CODE IN GRID.

	RESPON-DENT	PARTNER	BOTH	OTHER	NOT APPLIC.	(DON'T KNOW)
1. Clothes	1(38)	1(41)	1(44)	1(47)	0	9(50)
2. Education costs	1(39)	1(42)	1(45)	1(48)	0	9(51)
3. Leisure activities	1(40)	1(43)	1(46)	1(49)	0	9(52)

Now turn to page 17 of the self completion, and answer
Q.103.

Q.103 Who in your household would you say has ...
      a) the most time for their own leisure?
      b) most personal spending money?

Tick <u>one</u> box for <u>each</u> of a) and b).

Now answer Q.104

Q.104 Please tick the statement which comes closest to how
the most important decisions are made in your
household. Tick <u>one</u> box only.

NOW GO TO Q.108

IF NO HUSBAND OR PARTNER ASK Q.105a

Q.105a Have you had a family holiday in the last 12 months?

		(53)	
	YES	1	- ASK Q.105b
	NO	2	] GO TO
	(DON'T KNOW)	9	] Q.106

Q.105b How much did your last main family holiday cost, including spending money?

WRITE IN AMOUNT £ [ ][ ][ ][ ]   (54,57)

(DON'T KNOW)   9   (58)

Q.106 Do you save regularly?

	(59)
YES	1
NO	2
(DON'T KNOW)	9

Q.107 In the last year, have you ever had to fall behind in your payment of ... READ OUT EACH IN TURN AND CODE IN GRID.

	YES	NO	NOT APPLIC.	(DON'T KNOW)	
1. Your mortgage or rent	1	2	0	9	(60)
2. Your gas bills	1	2	0	9	(61)
3. Your electricity bills	1	2	0	9	(62)
4. Hire purchase payments	1	2	0	9	(63)

ALL RESPONDENTS

Q.108 CHECK MARITAL STATUS AT Q.74, AND CODE

		(64)	
CODE 1:	ALWAYS MARRIED	1	- GO TO Q.136a (P.40)
CODE 2:	ALWAYS COHABITING	2	- ASK Q.109
CODE 3:	FORMERLY COHABITING, NOW MARRIED	3	- GO TO Q.116 (P.32)
CODES 5 AND 7:	FORMERLY COHABITING	4	- GO TO Q.123 (P.35)
CODES 4 AND 6:	FORMERLY MARRIED	5	- GO TO Q.129 (P.38)

Q.109 I'd like to talk now about the relationship between your four year old
child ... (NAME) and your partner.

As you know, couples and their children change their circumstances
quite often nowadays. May I just check, is your present partner the
other parent of this child?

		(65)	
YES		1	- GO TO Q.110a
NO		2 ⌝	GO TO
(DON'T KNOW)		9 ⌟	Q.133 (P.38)

Q.110a Did you and your partner <u>jointly</u> register ... (CHILD)'s birth?

	(66)	
YES	1	- GO TO Q.111
NO	2	- ASK Q.110b
(DON'T KNOW)	9	- GO TO Q.111

Q.110b Why was that? **PROBE FULLY**

(67)	(68)
(69)	(70)
(71)	(72)
(73)	(74)

Q.111   Whose last name does .... (CHILD) use? **PROMPT WITH
PRECODES IF NECESSARY.**

	(75)
RESPONDENT'S	1
PARTNER'S/HUSBANDS	2
SOME COMBINATION OF BOTH	3
RESPONDENT, PARTNER AND CHILD ALL USE SAME NAME	4
OTHER (CODE AND WRITE IN)	5

- -

(76)

Q.112 Have you and your partner ever taken any steps to establish a <u>formal</u>
<u>or legal</u> relationship between him and ....(CHILD)? For example
have you ever ...
a) Gone to the courts for an order giving your partner
"parental rights"?

		(77)
	YES	1
	NO	2
	(DON'T KNOW)	9

b) Drawn up a formal legal agreement giving him
"parental responsibility"?

		(78)
	YES	1
	NO	2
	(DON'T KNOW)	9

c) Made some other written agreement between you?

		(79)
	YES	1
	NO	2
WRITE IN DETAILS	(DON'T KNOW)	9

(80) BLANK	CARD 10
(11)	(12)
(13)	(14)
(15)	(16)
(17)	(18)

_ _

_ _

_ _

d) Done anything else?

		(19)
	YES	1
	NO	2
WRITE IN DETAILS	(DON'T KNOW)	9

_ _

_ _

_ _

(20)	(21)
(22)	(23)
(24)	(25)
(26)	(27)

IF 'NO' AT Q.111 a,b, <u>and</u> c ASK Q.113. OTHERS GO TO
Q.114a.

Q.113 Why have you not taken steps to create a legal relationship between
your partner and your child? PROBE FULLY

(28)	(29)
(30)	(31)
(32)	(33)
(34)	(35)

Q.114a Do you ever feel under any pressure to get married?

		(36)	
	YES	1	] ASK
	UNCERTAIN	2	] Q.114b
	NO	3	- GO TO Q.115a

Q.114b Who is it that makes you feel under pressure? What do they do or say to make you feel that way?

(37)	(38)
(39)	(40)
(41)	(42)
(43)	(44)
(45)	(46)
(47)	(48)

Q.115a Do you think that not being legally married will affect your child(ren) in any way?

		(49)	
	YES	1	] ASK
	UNCERTAIN	2	] Q.115b
	NO	3	- GO TO Q.136a (P.40)

Q.115b In what way might your child(ren) be affected? PROBE FULLY

(50)	(51)
(52)	(53)
(54)	(55)
(56)	(57)
(58)	(59)
(60)	(61)

NOW GO PAGE 40 AND Q.136a

IF CODE 3 AT Q.108 - FORMERLY COHABITING, NOW
MARRIED - ASK Q.116

Q.116 I'd now like to talk about the relationship between your 4 year old
child ... (NAME) and your husband, before you got married.

As you know, couples and their children change their circumstances
quite often nowadays. May I just check, is your present husband the
other parent of this child?

		(62)
	YES	1 - ASK Q.117a
	NO	2 ⌉ GO TO
(DON'T KNOW)		9 ⌋ Q.133a

Q.117a Did you and your husband jointly register ... (CHILD'S) birth?

		(63)
	YES	1 - GO TO Q.118
	NO	2 - ASK Q.117b
(DON'T KNOW)		9 - GO TO Q.118

Q.117b Why was that? PROBE FULLY

(64)	(65)
(66)	(67)
(68)	(69)
(70)	(71)

Q.118 Whose last name does .... (CHILD) use? PROMPT WITH
PRECODES IF NECESSARY.

	(72)
RESPONDENT'S	1
PARTNER'S/HUSBANDS	2
SOME COMBINATION OF BOTH	3
RESPONDENT, PARTNER AND CHILD ALL USE SAME NAME	4
OTHER (CODE AND WRITE IN)	5

_ | (73) |

Q.119 Did you and your husband take any steps to establish a <u>formal or legal</u> relationship between him and your .... (CHILD) <u>before you got married?</u> Did you for example.....

a) Go to the courts for an order giving your partner "parental rights"?

	(74)
YES	1
NO	2
(DON'T KNOW)	9

b) Draw up a formal legal agreement giving him "parental responsibility"?

	(75)
YES	1
NO	2
(DON'T KNOW)	9

c) Make some other written agreement between you?

	(76)
YES	1
NO	2
(DON'T KNOW)	9

WRITE IN DETAILS

(77-80) BLANK | CARD 11

(11)	(12)
(13)	(14)
(15)	(16)
(17)	(18)

d) Do anything else?

	(19)
YES	1
NO	2
(DON'T KNOW)	9

WRITE IN DETAILS

(20)	(21)
(22)	(23)
(24)	(25)
(26)	(27)

IF 'NO' AT Q.119a,b,<u>AND</u> c ASK Q.120 (OTHERS GO TO Q.121a)

Q.120 Why did you not take any steps to create a legal relationship between your husband and your child <u>before you married</u>? PROBE FULLY

(28)	(29)
(30)	(31)
(32)	(33)
(34)	(35)

Q.121a Did you ever feel under any pressure to get married?

		(36)		
YES		1	]	ASK
UNCERTAIN		2	]	Q.121b
NO		3	-	GO TO Q.122a

Q.121b Who was it that made you feel under pressure? What did they do or say to make you feel that way?

(37)	(38)
(39)	(40)
(41)	(42)
(43)	(44)

Q.122a Do you think that not being legally married affected, or would have affected your child(ren) in any way?

	(45)		
YES	1	]	ASK
UNCERTAIN	2	]	Q.122b
NO	3	-	GO TO Q.136a (P.40)

Q.122b In way ways might your child(ren) have been affected? PROBE FULLY

(46)	(47)
(48)	(49)
(50)	(51)
(52)	(53)

NOW GO PAGE 40 AND Q.136a

IF CODES 5 OR 7 - FORMERLY COHABITING - AT Q.108 ASK Q.123

Q.123   I'd like to talk now about the relationship between your 4 year old child and the partner you were living with just after ..... (4 YR OLD CHILD) was born.

As you know, couples and their children change their circumstances quite often nowadays. May I just check, is your <u>former</u> partner the other parent of this child?

		(54)
YES		1 - ASK Q.124a
NO		2 ⌉ GO TO
(DON'T KNOW)		9 ⌋ Q.133a

Q.124a Did you and your partner <u>jointly</u> register ... (CHILD)'s birth?

	(55)
YES	1 - GO TO Q.125
NO	2 - ASK Q.124b
(DON'T KNOW)	9 - GO TO Q.125

Q.124b Why was that? PROBE FULLY

(56)	(57)
(58)	(59)
(60)	(61)
(62)	(63)

Q.125   Whose last name does .... (CHILD) use? PROMPT WITH PRECODES IF NECESSARY.

	(64)
RESPONDENT'S	1
PARTNER'S/HUSBANDS	2
SOME COMBINATION OF BOTH	3
RESPONDENT, PARTNER AND CHILD ALL USE SAME NAME	4
OTHER (CODE AND WRITE IN)	5

-                      (65)

Q.126   Did you and your partner take any steps to establish a <u>formal or legal</u>
        relationship between him and .... (CHILD) while you were living
        together or after you separated? Did you for example....

        a) Go to the courts for an order giving your partner
        "parental rights"?

	(66)
YES	1
NO	2
(DON'T KNOW)	9

        b) Draw up a formal legal agreement giving him
            "parental responsibility"?

	(67)
YES	1
NO	2
(DON'T KNOW)	9

        c) Make some other written agreement between you?

	(68)
YES	1
NO	2
(DON'T KNOW)	9

WRITE IN DETAILS

- -

(69)	(70)
(71)	(72)
(73)	(74)
(75)	(76)

        d) Do anything else?

	(77)
YES	1
NO	2
(DON'T KNOW)	9

WRITE IN DETAILS

- -

(78-80) BLANK	CARD 12
(11)	(12)
(13)	(14)
(15)	(16)
(17)	(18)

IF 'NO' AT Q.126a, b,<u>AND</u> c ASK Q.127. OTHERS GO TO
Q.128a

Q.127 Were there any reasons why you did not take steps to create a
       legal relationship between your partner and your child?
       PROBE FULLY

(19)	(20)
(21)	(22)
(23)	(24)
(25)	(26)

Q.128a Do you think that not being legally married might have
       contributed in any way to the breakdown of your relationship
       (with your former partner)?

```
                                         (27)
                            YES           1  ┐ ASK
                      UNCERTAIN           2  ┘ Q.128b
          -----------------------------------------------------
                             NO           3  -  GO TO Q.129a
```

Q.128b How do you think it might have contributed (to the breakdown
       of your relationship)? PROBE FULLY

(28)	(29)
(30)	(31)
(32)	(33)
(34)	(35)

IF NOT WITH ORIGINAL PARTNER (CODES 4-7 AT Q.74) ASK
Q.129. OTHERS GO TO Q.133

Q.129   Does your former partner/husband - contribute financially to ...
        (CHILD)'s care?

                                                                    (36)
                                                      YES   1 - ASK Q.130

                                                       NO   2 ⎤ GO TO
                                              (DON'T KNOW)   9 ⎦ Q.132a

Q.130   Do you have a formal (ie Legal) financial arrangement with him,
        or does he pay you money on an informal basis?

                                                                    (37)
                                       FORMAL ARRANGEMENT   1
                                     INFORMAL ARRANGEMENT   2
                                            (DON'T KNOW)   9

Q.131   Do you get your payments on a regular basis, or does he
        sometimes skip payments or send them late?

                                        PAYMENT REGULAR   1   (38)
                                        PAYMENTS SKIPPED   1   (39)
                                      PAYMENTS LATE/SLOW   1   (40)
                                        OTHER - WRITE IN   1   (41)

        -          (42)

        -          (43)

                                            (DON'T KNOW)   9   (44)

Q.132a Are you satisfied with the financial arrangements you have with
        your former partner/husband?

                                                                    (45)
                                                      YES   1 - GO TO Q.133

                                                       NO   2 - ASK Q.132b
        ----
                                              (DON'T KNOW)   9 - GO TO Q.133

Q.132b In what way are you dissatisfied? PROBE FULLY

(46)	(47)
(48)	(49)
(50)	(51)
(52)	(53)

        IF NOT LIVING WITH 4 YEAR OLD'S FATHER ASK Q.133
        (OTHERS GO TO Q.136a)

Q.133   How far away does ... (CHILD)'s father live? Does he, for
        example ... READ OUT AND CODE ONE ANSWER OR RECORD
        MILEAGE

                                                                    (54)
                   live within walking distance of your home   1
                           live within the same village/town   2
                        live in another part of the same county   3
                           live in another part of the country   4
                                 live in another country   5
                                            (DON'T KNOW)   9

        OR
                   DISTANCE [| | |] MILES   (55-58)

Q.134a Does your former partner/husband maintain contact with ...
(CHILD)?

	(59)
YES	1 - ASK Q.134b
NO	2 - GO TO Q.135

Q.134b **SHOW CARD 6:** How often does he see him/her?

	(60)	
MORE THAN ONCE A WEEK	1	
ONCE A WEEK	2	
ONCE A FORTNIGHT	3	GO
MONTHLY	4	TO
OTHER - SPECIFY	5	Q.136
_ _ _ _ _ _ _ _ _ _ _ _ _ _ _ _ _ _ _		
(DON'T KNOW)	9	

(61)

IF 'NO' AT Q.134a ASK Q.135
Q.135 Why do you think he has lost contact with him/her?
PROBE FULLY

(62)	(63)
(64)	(65)
(66)	(67)
(68)	(69)

```
┌─────────────────────────┐
│   BACKGROUND DETAILS    │
└─────────────────────────┘
```

ASK ALL
I'd now like to ask you a few background questions which will help us understand what your family is like in comparison with other families.

Q.136a When you were aged about 14, what was your father's job title? WRITE IN JOB TITLE. PROMPT FOR FULL DETAILS OF WORK DONE. IF NO JOB, CODE REASON

(70) - (73)

WRITE IN FULL
JOB TITLE: _

PROMPT FOR FULL DETAILS OF WORK DONE: _ _ _ _ _ _ _ _ _ _ _ _   ⎤
                                                                     ⎬ ASK Q.136b
_   ⎟
                                                                     ⎦
_ _

                                                OR: (74)
                                          NO FATHER   1 ⎤
┌──────────────────────────┐   UNEMPLOYED   2 ⎬ SKIP TO Q.138a
│ N.B. IF WAS LIVING WITH │   RETIRED   3 ⎟
│ STEPFATHER AT AGE 14 GET │   (DON'T KNOW)   8 ⎦
│ DETAILS OF STEPFATHER'S JOB │
└──────────────────────────┘
```

Q.136b SHOW CARD 7  Which group on this card best describes his position in that job at that time (that is, when you were 14)?  Just read out the number beside the appropriate one.

```
                                                              (75)
                1. SELF-EMPLOYED WITH 25 OR MORE EMPLOYEES     1
                2. SELF-EMPLOYED WITH LESS THAN 25 EMPLOYEES   2
                3. SELF-EMPLOYED WITHOUT EMPLOYEES             3
        ----------------------------------------------------------
        4. MANAGER IN ESTABLISHMENT WITH 25 OR MORE PERSONS    4
        5. MANAGER IN ESTABLISHMENT WITH LESS THAN 25 PERSONS  5
        ----------------------------------------------------------
                            6. FOREMAN OR SUPERVISOR           6
                            7. OTHER EMPLOYEE OR APPRENTICE     7
        ----------------------------------------------------------
                                       (DON'T KNOW)            8
```

(76)

(77) - (79)

Q.137 What did the firm or organisation he worked for actually make or do at the place where he worked? WRITE IN DETAILS.

(80) BLANK

_ _

_ _

_ _
```

Q.138a Did your (step) mother work outside the home at any time when you were growing up?

YES	(11) 1	- ASK Q.138b

NO	2	GO TO
NO MOTHER	3	FILTER ABOVE
(DON'T KNOW	9	Q.139a

Q.138b What type of work did she do when you were aged about 14?
PROMPT FOR FULL DETAILS

(12 - 15)

(16 - 18)

Q.138c Did she mainly work part-time or full-time?

	(19)
PART-TIME	1
FULL-TIME	2
MIXED PART AND FULL TIME	3
(DON'T KNOW)	9

IF RESPONDENT IS CURRENTLY EMPLOYED (Q.2) ASK
Q.139a. OTHERS GO TO Q.140
Q.139a What was your last take-home pay, after deductions for tax, national insurance and superannuation? ENTER FIGURE INTO BOXES USING LEADING ZERO IF NECESSARY.

NET PAY ----> £ | (20) | (21) | (22) | (23) |

	(24)	
OR: (REFUSED)	7	GO TO
(DON'T KNOW)	8	Q.140

Q.139b What period did this cover?

	(25)
ONE WEEK	1
TWO WEEKS	2
FOUR WEEKS	3
CALENDAR MONTH	4
ANNUAL	5
OTHER (WRITE IN AND CODE 6)	
	6

| (26) |

Q.139c Did you have any earnings from any other jobs during this same period?

	(27)	
YES	1	- ASK Q.139d
NO	2	- GO TO Q.140

Q.139d How much did these other earnings come to in total (after any deductions for tax, national insurance and superannuation)?
ENTER FIGURE INTO BOXES USING LEADING ZEROS IF NECESSARY.

NET OTHER EARNINGS --> £ | | | | | (28-31)

	(32)
OR: (REFUSED)	7
(DON'T KNOW)	8

Q.140 Do you (or your employer) contribute towards an occupational
pension or a personal pension plan (in addition to the state
pension)?

	(33)
YES	1
NO	2
(DON'T KNOW)	9

ALL RESPONDENTS
Q.141 CHECK MARITAL STATUS AT Q.74

	(34)
CODES 1-5 - WITH PARTNER	1 - ASK Q.142a
CODES 6 OR 7 - NO PARTNER	2 - GO TO FILTER AT Q.155

Q.142a Is your partner currently working?

	(35)
CURRENTLY WORKING	1 - ASK Q.142b
NOT EMPLOYED AT PRESENT	2 - GO TO Q.144

Q.142b Is he self-employed?

	(36)
YES	1
NO	2
(DON'T KNOW)	9

Q.143 What is the title of his job? PROMPT FOR FULL DETAILS OF
WORK DONE

(37 - 40)

(41 - 43)

NOW GO TO Q.147

IF PARTNER NOT EMPLOYED ASK Q.144
Q.144 What is your partner's current position? Is he......
READ OUT

		(44)
unemployed	1	- ASK Q.145
a student	2	
retired	3	GO TO
Other - write in	4	Q.147
(DON'T KNOW)	9	

(45)

Q.145 How long has your partner been unemployed?

WRITE IN [ ][ ] MONTHS   (46,47)

OR CODE

(48)
LESS THAN 1 MONTH   1
(DON'T KNOW)   9

Q.146 What was the title of the last job he had?
PROMPT FOR DETAILS OF WORK DONE

(49)
NEVER HAD A JOB   1

JOB TITLE: _____   (50-53)

WORK DONE: _____   (54-56)

_____

┌─────────────────────────────────┐
│   ASK ALL WITH PARTNER   │
└─────────────────────────────────┘

Q.147 How old was your partner on his last birthday?

(57)
WRITE IN AGE [ ][ ]   (58)

(DON'T KNOW)   9 (59)

┌──┐
│ Now turn to page 18 of the self completion and answer Q.138 │
│   │
│ Q.148 We are interested in how you get along with your   │
│   husband or partner. Please answer the questions on │   ✱
│   page 18 and and then turn over to page 19 and answer │
│   questions 150-154.   │
│   │
│ CHECK WITH RESPONDENT THAT THEY HAVE ANSWERED THE LAST PAGE │
│ OF SELF-COMPLETION   │
└──┘

ASK ALL

Q.155 SHOW CARD 8 - EXPLAIN ABOUT 3 VERSIONS Thinking of all
the members of your household who have income from any
source, including yourself, into which of the categories on this
card would you estimate (your/your household's) usual total net
income falls, that is, after deductions for tax and national
insurance. You should think of all sources of income, from any
investments, benefits or pensions as well as from work. Just
read out the letter beside the appropriate group.

		(60)
AFTER CODING CHECK:	G	1
	C	2
(i) IS FOR ALL HOUSEHOLD MEMBERS,	B	3
INCLUDING RESPONDENT.	P	4
	L	5
(ii) IS A NET SUM (NOT GROSS)	T	6
	E	7
(iii) INCLUDES ALL SOURCES OF INCOME	A	8
(NOT JUST FROM WORK).	S	9

		(61)
AMEND CATEGORY IF NECESSARY		
	H	1
	R	2
	D	3
	K	4
	N	5
	V	6
(REFUSED)		7
(DON'T KNOW)		8

THANK RESPONDENT AND CLOSE
REMEMBER TO TAKE BACK SELF-COMPLETION

TIME INTERVIEW ENDED [| | |]

(62 - 65)

PAS 12867/RL

A STUDY OF WOMEN WITH CHILDREN

Self Completion Questionnaire

- Please answer the questions by ticking ☑ the box(es) beside the appropriate answer(s).

- You do not need to answer all the questions - the interviewer will tell you which to answer.

- Do not turn pages or answer any questions until the interviewer asks you to do so.

- If you have any problems, please ask the interview for help.

NAME: _____ ☐ ☐ ☐ ☐ (11-14)

Q.16 We are interested in the reasons why you are currently
working in a paid job. Would you please tick those things
which were important in influencing your decision to work at
this time.

| PLEASE TICK ALL THE REASONS THAT APPLY TO YOU |

Working is the normal thing to do ☐ 1   (15)

I need the money for basic essentials such as food,
rent or mortgage payments ☐ 1   (16)

My children are old enough to leave/don't need my
full-time care and attention ☐ 1   (17)

I enjoy working ☐ 1   (18)

I like the company of other people ☐ 1   (19)

In order to earn money for extras ☐ 1   (20)

In order to earn money of my own ☐ 1   (21)

To follow my career ☐ 1   (22)

Some other important factors - please write in ☐ 1   (23)

_   (24,25)

_   (26,27)

(28,29)

(30,31)

Q.23 We are interested in the reasons why you are <u>not</u> currently working in a paid job. Please tick those things which were important in influencing <u>your decision not to work at this time</u>.

| PLEASE TICK ALL THE REASONS THAT APPLY TO YOU |

I prefer not to work ☐ 1 (32)

My child's health prevents me from working ☐ 1 (33)

My partner prefers me not to work ☐ 1 (34)

I cannot find a paid job ☐ 1 (35)

I cannot find a paid job with convenient hours or in a convenient location ☐ 1 (36)

I think that mothers with young children should not work outside the home ☐ 1 (37)

I cannot earn enough to pay for childcare ☐ 1 (38)

I cannot find suitable childcare ☐ 1 (39)

I am caring for elderly/ill relative or friend ☐ 1 (40)

I am in full-time education or training ☐ 1 (41)

My health or disability prevents me from working ☐ 1 (42)

Some other important reasons - please write in ☐ 1 (43)

_ (44,45)
(46,47)
_ (48,49)
(50,51)

Q.33   We are interested in why you and your husband set up home
       together when you did. Please tick those things which were
       important in influencing the point in your life when you first
       set up home together.

> PLEASE TICK ALL THE REASONS THAT APPLY TO YOU

I couldn't stand living in my previous household any more ☐ 1 (52)

We fell in love, and could not live without each other ☐ 1 (53)

I was pregnant ☐ 1 (54)

We'd got enough money together to get a house ☐ 1 (55)

Rented accommodation became available ☐ 1 (56)

My previous household was splitting up ☐ 1 (57)

The time had come when I wanted to live with a regular sexual partner ☐ 1 (58)

I was at a suitable point in my working life ☐ 1 (59)

My partner was at a suitable point in his working life ☐ 1 (60)

We wanted to have a child ☐ 1 (61)

Some other important factors - please write in ☐ 1 (62)

- (63,64)
                                                                  (65,66)
- (67,68)
                                                                  (69,70)

Q.37 **We are interested in why you and your husband decided to get married. Please tick all those things which were important in influencing your decision to get married.**

| PLEASE TICK ALL THE THINGS THAT APPLY TO YOU |

I wanted the security of being married ☐ 1 (71)

I wanted to make my children more secure ☐ 1 (72)

All my friends were getting married and I thought it was about time I did too ☐ 1 (73)

We fell in love, and could not live without each other ☐ 1 (74)

We'd got enough money together to get a house ☐ 1 (75)

It was important to my/my partner's parents that we got married ☐ 1 (76)

I was pregnant ☐ 1 (77)

I wanted to get married for religious reasons ☐ 1 (78)

We wanted to have a child ☐ 1 (79)

We wanted to make a public/further commitment to each other ☐ 1 (80)

CARD 15

My children wanted me to get married ☐ 1 (11)

I/my partner became legally free to get married again ☐ 1 (12)

Some other important factors - please write in ☐ 1 (13)

_ (14,15)
(16,17)
_ (18,19)
(20,21)

Q.38 We are interested in why you and your husband decided to get married. Please tick all those things which were important in influencing your decision to get married.

| PLEASE TICK ALL THE REASONS THAT APPLY TO YOU |

I wanted the security of being married [ ] 1 (22)

I wanted to make my children more secure [ ] 1 (23)

All my friends were getting married and I thought it was about time I did too [ ] 1 (24)

We fell in love, and could not live without each other [ ] 1 (25)

We'd got enough money together to get a house [ ] 1 (26)

It was important to my/my partner's parents that we got married [ ] 1 (27)

I was pregnant [ ] 1 (28)

I wanted to get married for religious reasons [ ] 1 (29)

We wanted to have a child [ ] 1 (30)

We wanted to make a public/further commitment to each other [ ] 1 (31)

My children wanted me to get married [ ] 1 (32)

I/my partner became legally free to get married again [ ] 1 (33)

Some other important factors - please write in [ ] 1 (34)

- (35,36)
                                                                      (37,38)
- (39,40)
                                                                      (41,42)

Q.52 We are interested in why you and your partner set up home together when you did. Please tick those things which were important in influencing the point in your life when you first set up home together.

> PLEASE TICK ALL THE REASONS THAT APPLY TO YOU

I couldn't stand living in my previous household any more ☐ 1 (43)

We fell in love, and could not live without each other ☐ 1 (44)

I was pregnant ☐ 1 (45)

We'd got enough money together to get a house ☐ 1 (46)

Rented accommodation became available ☐ 1 (47)

My previous household was splitting up ☐ 1 (48)

The time had come when I wanted to live with a regular sexual partner ☐ 1 (49)

I was at a suitable point in my working life ☐ 1 (50)

My partner was at a suitable point in his working life ☐ 1 (51)

We wanted to have a child ☐ 1 (52)

Some other important factors - please write in ☐ 1 (53)

- (54,55)
(56,57)
- (58,59)
(60,61)

Q.57 We are interested in what things might be important in influencing your decision to get married someday. Please tick all those things that might be important in influencing your decision.

┌───┐
│ **PLEASE TICK ALL THE REASONS THAT APPLY TO YOU** │
└───┘

My personal security ☐ 1 (62)

My children's security ☐ 1 (63)

The wishes of my parents/my partner's parents ☐ 1 (64)

My children's wishes ☐ 1 (65)

Wanting to make a public/further commitment to each other ☐ 1 (66)

Some other important factors - please write in ☐ 1 (67)

_ (68,69)
(70,71)
_ (72,73)
(74,75)

Q.61 We are interested in why you and your partner set up home together when you did. Please tick those things which were important in influencing the point in your life when you first set up home together.

> | PLEASE TICK ALL THE REASONS THAT APPLY TO YOU |

I couldn't stand living in my previous household any more ☐ 1 (11)

We fell in love, and could not live without each other ☐ 1 (12)

I was pregnant ☐ 1 (13)

We'd got enough money together to get a house ☐ 1 (14)

Rented accommodation became available ☐ 1 (15)

My previous household was splitting up ☐ 1 (16)

The time had come when I wanted to live with a regular sexual partner ☐ 1 (17)

I was at a suitable point in my working life ☐ 1 (18)

My partner was at a suitable point in his working life ☐ 1 (19)

We wanted to have a child ☐ 1 (20)

Some other important factors - please write in ☐ 1 (21)

_ (22,23)
(24,25)
_ (26,27)
(28,29)

Q.66 We are interested in why you and your husband decided to get married. Please tick all those things which were important in influencing your decision to get married.

┌───┐
│ PLEASE TICK ALL THE REASONS THAT APPLY TO YOU │
└───┘

I wanted the security of being married ☐ 1 (30)

I wanted to make my children more secure ☐ 1 (31)

All my friends were getting married and I thought it was about time I did too ☐ 1 (32)

We fell in love, and could not live without each other ☐ 1 (33)

We'd got enough money together to get a house ☐ 1 (34)

It was important to my/my partner's parents that we got married ☐ 1 (35)

I was pregnant ☐ 1 (36)

I wanted to get married for religious reasons ☐ 1 (37)

We wanted to have a child ☐ 1 (38)

We wanted to make a public/further commitment to each other ☐ 1 (39)

My children wanted me to get married ☐ 1 (40)

I/my partner became legally free to get married again ☐ 1 (41)

Some other important factors - please write in ☐ 1 (42)

_ (43,44)
(45,46)
_ (47,58)
(49,50)

Q.78   Would you please tick those things which were important in
        influencing the point in your life when you had your first
        child?

┌───┐
│ PLEASE TICK ALL THE REASONS THAT APPLY TO YOU │
└───┘

I became pregnant unexpectedly ☐ 1 (51)

I'd always planned to start a family at that time ☐ 1 (52)

I wanted to start a family before I was too old ☐ 1 (53)

I felt the time had come when we could manage on only one income
for a while ☐ 1 (54)

I was fed up with working and wanted a change ☐ 1 (55)

I lost my job, which gave me the chance to start a family ☐ 1 (56)

I thought it would make life more interesting ☐ 1 (57)

I knew my parents would be very disappointed if I didn't ☐ 1 (58)

We thought we were then in a position to give a child the
time and attention he/she deserved ☐ 1 (59)

Some other important factors - please write in ☐ 1 (60)

                                                        (61,62)
-   (63,64)
                                                        (65,66)
-   (67,68)

┌───┐
│   NOW TURN OVER AND ANSWER Q.79 │
└───┘

Q.79 **Please tick the description which applies to you, and then answer one question from the following two pages, according to the instructions given.**

> | TICK ONE BOX ONLY |

(69)

A.	I have a child/children and <u>hope</u> to have more	☐ → GO TO Q.80 ON PAGE 12	1
B.	I have a child/children but <u>hope</u> <u>not</u> to have any more	☐ → GO TO Q.81 ON PAGE 13	2

PLEASE ANSWER Q.80 IF YOU HOPE TO HAVE MORE CHILDREN

Q.80   Would you please tick any of the following list of reasons why
you expect to have more children in the future.

PLEASE TICK ALL THE REASONS THAT APPLY TO YOU

I am pregnant at the moment ☐ 1 (70)

I like children, and enjoy having them around me ☐ 1 (71)

I think we can afford at least one child more than we have at present ☐ 1 (72)

I feel it is one's duty to have as many children as one can ☐ 1 (73)

I see my main role in life as wife and mother ☐ 1 (74)

It would give me a sense of doing something worthwhile when
there are no suitable jobs available ☐ 1 (75)

I could still give any further children the time and attention
they need ☐ 1 (76)

It would be company for my previous child(ren) ☐ 1 (77)

It is wrong to try to plan how many children you have ☐ 1 (78)

My life would be richer with more children ☐ 1 (79)

To look after me in my old age ☐ 1 (80)

CARD 17

My previous children are all boys and I'd like a girl ☐ 1 (11)

My previous children are all girls and I'd like a boy ☐ 1 (12)

Some other important factors - please write in ☐ 1 (13)

- (14,15)
(16,17)
- (18,19)
(20,21)

PLEASE ANSWER Q.81 IF YOU DO <u>NOT</u> INTEND TO HAVE MORE CHILDREN

Q.81   Please tick any of the following list of reasons why you
<u>originally</u> came to the view that you would not have any more
children.

PLEASE TICK ALL THE REASONS THAT APPLY TO YOU

I couldn't have any more children ☐ 1 (22)

My health or age meant that it wasn't a good idea to try to have more children ☐ 1 (23)

I was happy with the number of children I had and did not want any more, even if I could have easily afforded it ☐ 1 (24)

I didn't think I could afford any more children ☐ 1 (25)

I have my hands full with the children I have ☐ 1 (26)

More children would have interfered with my work plans ☐ 1 (27)

I didn't want to bring any more children into such an uncertain world ☐ 1 (28)

My partner didn't want any more ☐ 1 (29)

My experience of childbirth and looking after a baby had put me off ☐ 1 (30)

I didn't think I could give my existing children the time and attention they deserved if I had any more ☐ 1 (31)

Some other important factors - please write in ☐ 1 (32)

_ (33,34)
(35,36)
_ (37,38)
(39,40)

Q.90 We are interested in who <u>usually</u> does the household tasks in your household. Please tick the box that describes how each of the following tasks is divided up or shared between you and your partner.

> TICK ONE BOX FOR EACH OF 1 - 9

	FEMALE PARTNER ALMOST ENTIRELY	FEMALE PARTNER MAINLY	BOTH EQUALLY	MALE PARTNER MAINLY	MALE PARTNER ALMOST ENTIRELY	NEITHER OF US DO THIS	NOT APPLI-CABLE	
1. Washing up	1	2	3	4	5	6	0	(41)
2. Hoovering, cleaning the house	1	2	3	4	5	6	0	(42)
3. Painting and decorating	1	2	3	4	5	6	0	(43)
4. Washing clothes	1	2	3	4	5	6	0	(44)
5. Gardening	1	2	3	4	5	6	0	(45)
6. Cooking for the family	1	2	3	4	5	6	0	(46)
7. Looking after/ maintaining the car	1	2	3	4	5	6	0	(47)
8. Taking children to doctor or hospital/ outpatients	1	2	3	4	5	6	0	(48)
9. Helping children with homework	1	2	3	4	5	6	0	(49)

Q.91 Does anyone else inside or outside your household usually help
you with these tasks?

| TICK ALL THAT APPLY |

	INSIDE HOUSEHOLD				OUTSIDE HOUSEHOLD			
	MALE CHILD IN HOUSE-HOLD	FEMALE CHILD IN HOUSE-HOLD	OTHER MALE IN HOUSE-HOLD	OTHER FEMALE IN HOUSE HOLD	UNPAID LABOUR FROM OUTSIDE HOUSE-HOLD	PAID LABOUR FROM OUTSIDE HOUSE-HOLD	NO-ONE ELSE HELPS	NOT APPLIC-ABLE	
1. Washing up	1	1	1	1	1	1	1	1	(50-57)
2. Hoovering, cleaning the house	1	1	1	1	1	1	1	1	(58-65)
3. Painting and decorating	1	1	1	1	1	1	1	1	(66-73) (74-80)
4. Washing clothes	1	1	1	1	1	1	1	1	BLANK (11-18)
5. Gardening	1	1	1	1	1	1	1	1	(19-26)
6. Cooking for the family	1	1	1	1	1	1	1	1	(27-34)
7. Looking after/maintaining the car	1	1	1	1	1	1	1	1	(35-42)
8. Taking children to doctor or hospital/ outpatients	1	1	1	1	1	1	1	1	(43-50)
9. Helping children with homework	1	1	1	1	1	1	1	1	(51-58)

Q.95a Thinking of your situation now, please tick the box which best describes who <u>in your household has ultimate</u> responsibility for each of the following.

| TICK ONE BOX FOR EACH OF 1-4 |

	MALE PARTNER	FEMALE PARTNER	BOTH EQUALLY	(DON'T KNOW)	
1. Ensuring that the housework is done properly	☐ 1	☐ 2	☐ 3	☐ 9	(59)
2. Ensuring that the family gets an adequate income	☐ 1	☐ 2	☐ 3	☐ 9	(60)
3. Looking after the children	☐ 1	☐ 2	☐ 3	☐ 9	(61)
4. Organising the household money and paying the bills	☐ 1	☐ 2	☐ 3	☐ 9	(62)

Q.95b And please tick the box which best describes who you think <u>should</u> have ultimate responsibility for each of the following.

| TICK ONE BOX FOR EACH OF 1-4 |

	MALE PARTNER	FEMALE PARTNER	BOTH EQUALLY	(DON'T KNOW)	
1. Ensuring that the housework is done properly	☐ 1	☐ 2	☐ 3	☐ 9	(63)
2. Ensuring that the family gets an adequate income	☐ 1	☐ 2	☐ 3	☐ 9	(64)
3. Looking after the children	☐ 1	☐ 2	☐ 3	☐ 9	(65)
4. Organising the household money and paying the bills	☐ 1	☐ 2	☐ 3	☐ 9	(66)

Q.103 Who in your household would you say has ....

> TICK ONE BOX FOR EACH

	MALE PARTNER	FEMALE PARTNER	BOTH THE SAME	
a) The most time for their own leisure	☐ 1	☐ 2	☐ 3	(67)
b) The most personal spending money	☐ 1	☐ 2	☐ 3	(68)

Q.104 Please tick the statement which comes closest to how the most important decisions are made in your household.

> TICK ONE BOX ONLY

(69)

The man has a lot more say over the most important decisions ☐ 1

The man has somewhat more say over the most important decisions ☐ 2

We both have an equal say over the most important decisions ☐ 3

The woman has somewhat more say over the most important decisions ☐ 4

The woman has a lot more say over the most important decisions ☐ 5

The final questions are about your current relationship with your partner.

Q.148 How happy is your relationship, all things considered?

| PLEASE TICK THE BOX WHICH BEST DESCRIBES HOW |
| HAPPY OR UNHAPPY YOU ARE BEING WITH YOUR |
| PARTNER |

Extremely happy		Neither happy nor unhappy				Extremely unhappy
□ 1	□ 2	□ 3	□ 4	□ 5	□ 6	□ 7 (70)

Q.149 Most people have disagreements with their partner. Please show how much you and your partner AGREE or DISAGREE about the things listed below.

| TICK ONE BOX FOR EACH ITEM |

	We nearly always agree	We often agree	We some-times agree, sometimes disagree	We often disagree	We nearly always disagree	We never talk about it	
1. Handling family finances	□1	□2	□3	□4	□5	□6	(71)
2. How to spend your spare time	□1	□2	□3	□4	□5	□6	(72)
3. Showing affection for each other	□1	□2	□3	□4	□5	□6	(73)
4. Liking the same friends	□1	□2	□3	□4	□5	□6	(74)
5. Having sex together	□1	□2	□3	□4	□5	□6	(75)
6. Behaving generally in the right and decent way towards other people	□1	□2	□3	□4	□5	□6	(76)
7. Sharing household tasks	□1	□2	□3	□4	□5	□6	(77)
8. Outlook on life	□1	□2	□3	□4	□5	□6	(78)
9. Relationships with parents parents-in-law	□1	□2	□3	□4	□5	□6	(79)
10. Deciding if or when to have children	□1	□2	□3	□4	□5	□6	(80)
11. How children should be brought up	□1	□2	□3	□4	□5	□6	(11)

| NOW TURN THE PAGE AND ANSWER Q.150-154 |

Q.150 When disagreements arise between you and your partner how do
they usually end?

TICK ONE BOX ONLY

(12)

You give in ☐ 1

Your partner gives in ☐ 2

Agreement by mutual give and take ☐ 3

You both agree to differ ☐ 4

Varies/depends/don't know ☐ 5

Q.151 Do you and your partner share any outside interests?

TICK ONE BOX ONLY

(13)

Yes, we share all our outside interests ☐ 1

Yes we share some outside interests ☐ 2

Yes we share a few outside interests ☐ 3

No, we don't share any outside interests ☐ 4

Q.152 Do you ever wish you had not married (or lived together as a
couple)?

TICK ONE BOX ONLY

(14)

Yes, frequently ☐ 1

Yes, occasionally ☐ 2

Only rarely ☐ 3

No, never ☐ 4

Q.153 If you had to live your life over again, which of these do you think
you would do?

TICK ONE BOX ONLY

(15)

Marry (or live as a couple with) the same person ☐ 1

Marry (or live as a couple with) a different person ☐ 2

Not marry (or live as a couple) at all ☐ 3

Don't know ☐ 4

Q.154 Do you share your problems with your partner?

TICK ONE BOX ONLY

(16)

Yes, I share all of them ☐ 1

Yes, I share most of them ☐ 2

Yes, I share some of them ☐ 3

No, I share none or hardly any of them ☐ 4

Bibliography

Agell, Anders, *Cohabitation without Marriage*, Stockholm: Liber, 1985.

Anderson, Michael, Bechhofer, Frank and Steve Kendrick, 'Individual and Household Strategies: Some Empirical Evidence from The SCELI', manuscript, no date.

Anderson, Olive, 'The Incidence of Civil Marriage in Victorian England and Wales', *Past and Present*, Vol 69, No.50.

Bernard, Jessie, *The Future of Marriage*, Bantam Books 1972 (4th edition 1978).

Bott, Elizabeth, *Family and Social Network*, Tavistock, 1957.

Bower, D. and V. Christopherson, 'University student cohabitation: a regional comparison of selected attitudes and behaviour', *Journal of Marriage and the Family*, 39, 1977.

Bowler, J., Jackson, J. and E. Loughridge, *Living Together: You, Your Partner and the Law*, Century, London, 1991.

Bradshaw, Jonathan and Jane Millar, *Lone Parent Families in the UK*, HMSO 1992.

Bromley's Family Law, 1976.

Brown, Joan, *Why don't they go to work? Mothers on benefit*, Social Security Advisory Committee, HMSO, 1989.

Burgoyne, J., *Cohabitation and Contemporary Family Life*, ESRC End of Grant Report, unpublished, 1985.

Centre National d'Information et de Documentation des Femmes et des Familles (CNIDFF), *Le Concubinage vos Droits*, Paris, 1992.

Chappell, Helen, 'Not the Marrying Kind?', *New Society*, 20 May 1982.

Cherlin, Andrew, 'Changing Family and Household: Contemporary Lessons from Historical Research', *American Sociological Review*, 9. 1983.

Clayton R. and H. Voss, 'Shacking up: Cohabitation in the 1970s', *Journal of Marriage and the Family*, 39, 1977.

Cretney, S.M. and J.M. Masson, *Principles of Family Law, 5th Edition*, Sweet and Maxwell, London, 1990.

Cunningham, J.D. and J.K. Anthill, 'Cohabitation: Marriage of the Future', Paper presented at the ANZAAS Congress, Aukland, NZ, 1979.

Davidoff, Leonore and Catherine Hall, *Family Fortunes: Men and Women of the English Middle Class 1780-1850*, Hutchinson, 1987.

Delphy, Christine and Diane Leonard, *Familiar Exploitation: A New Analysis of Marriage in Contemporary Western Societies*, Polity Press, 1992.

Donovan, K., *Sexual Divisions in Law*, London: Weidenfeld and Nicolson, 1985.

Dunnell, Karen, *Family Formation Survey*, London, HMSO, 1979.

Employment Gazette, 'Women and the labour market: results from the 1991 Labour Force Survey', September 1992, Table 6, corrected October 1992.

Ermisch, John, *Fewer Babies, Longer Lives*, York: Joseph Rowntree Memorial Trust, 1990.

European Observatory on Family Policies, *Families and Policies: Trends and Developments in 1988-89*, Final Report, 1990.

European Observatory on National Family Policies, Families and Policies: Evolutions and Trends, 1989-1990, EC, 1992.

Fielding, W.J., *Strange Customs of Courtship and Marriage*, London: Souvenir Press, 1961.

Gershuny, Jonathan, 'Change in the domestic division of labour in the UK, 1975-1987: dependent labour versus adaptive partnership', in N. Abercrombie and A. Warde (eds) *Social Change in Contemporary Britain*, Polity Press, Cambridge, 1982.

Gillis, John R, *For Better, For Worse: British Marriages, 1600 to the Present*, Oxford University Press, 1985.

Gittens, Diana, *The Family in Question: Changing Households and Familiar Ideologies, 2nd Edition*, Macmillan, 1993.

Glendon, Mary Ann, 'The New Marriage and the New Property' in John Eekelaar and S. Katz, *Marriage and Cohabitation in Contemporary Socities*, Toronto, 1980.

Haskey, John, *Population Trends*, No 68, Summer 1992.

Haskey, John and David Coleman, 'Cohabitation before marriage: a comparison of information from marriage registration and the GHS', *Population Trends*, No. 43 (Spring) 1986.

Haskey, J. and K. Kiernan, 'Cohabitation in Great Britain – characteristics and estimated numbers of cohabiting partners', *Population Trends*, 58, Winter 1989.

Haskey, John and Sue Kelly, 'Population estimates by cohabitation and legal marital status – a trial of new estimates', *Population Trends*, 60 Winter 1991.

Hoem, Britta, 'One child is not enough: What has happened to Swedish women with one child born in 1936-60?', *Stockholm Research Reports in Demography, No. 25, Stockholm: University of Stockholm, 1985.*

Jones, W.R., 'Living Tally', MS 259/24, Welsh Folk Museum.

Jones, W.R., 'Lore of Courtship and Marriage', Jones MSS 236, fol. 96.

Jones, W.R., 'A Besom Wedding in the Ceiriog Valley', *Folklore*, XXXIX, 1928.

Joseph, George, *Women at Work*, London: Philip Allen, 1983.

Joseph Rowntree Foundation, 'The effect of housing costs on young people's lifestyles', *Housing Research Findings* No 68, October 1992.

Khoo, S-E., 'Living Together as Married: A profile of de facto couples in Australia', *Journal of Marriage and the Family*, 49, 1987.

Kiernan, K., 'Changing marriage patterns', *Journal of Social Work Practice*, Vol 5, No 2, 1991.

Kiernan, Kathleen, 'The roles of men and women in tomorrow's Europe', *Employment Gazette*, October 1992.

Kiernan, Kathleen and Malcolm Wicks, *Family change and future policy*, York: Joseph Rowntree Memorial Trust in association with the Family Policy Studies Centre, June 1990.

Kiernan, Kathleen and Valerie Estaugh, *Cohabitation Extra-Marital Childbearing and Social Policy*, Family Policy Studies Centre, 1993.

Land, Hilary, *Women and Economic Dependency*, Equal Opportunities Commission, 1986.

Lasch, Christopher, 'The Suppression of Clandestine Marriage in England: The Marriage Act of 1753', *Salmagundi*, No. 26, Spring 1974.

Mansfield, Penny and Jean Collard, *The Beginning of the Rest of your Life?*, Macmillan, 1988.

McRae, Susan, *Maternity Rights in Britain: The experience of women and employers*, London: Policy Studies Institute, 1991.

Menefee, S.P., *Wives for Sale*, Oxford: Blackwell Books, 1981.

Millar, Jane, 'Lone Mothers' in C Glendinning and Jane Millar (eds), *Women and Poverty in Britain*, Wheatsheaf, 1987.

Oliver, Dawn, 'Why Do People Live Together?', *Journal of Social Welfare Law*, 1982.

Outhwaite, R.B., *Marriage and Society: Studies in the Social History of Marriage*, London: Europa, 1980.

Parker, Stephen, *Informal Marriage, Cohabitation and the Law, 1750-1989*, Macmillan, 1990.

Pinchbeck, I., *Women Workers and Industrial Revolution*, Virago, 1981.

Popenoe, David, 'Beyond the Nuclear Family: A statistical portrait of the changing family in Sweden', *Journal of Marriage and the Family*, 49, February 1987.

Population Trends, 1991.

Priest, Jacqueline, *Families Outside Marriage*, Family Law/Jordan and Sons, Bristol, 1990.

Risman, B., Hill, C.T., Rubin Z. and L.A. Peplau, 'Living together in college: implications for courtship', *Journal of Marriage and the Family,* 43, 1981.

Roll, Jo, *Lone Parents in the European Community*, Family Policy Studies Centre, 1992.

Sarantakos, S. *Living together* in Australia, Melbourne: Longman Chesire, 1984.

Social Trends, 1991.

Stafford, R., Blackman, E. and P. Dibona, 'The division of labor among cohabiting and married couples, *Journal of Marriage and the Family*, 39, 1977.

Tilly, Louise and Joan Scott, *Women, Work and Family*, New York: Holt, Rhinehart and Winston: 1978.